BY THE HAND OR BY THE PEN

An Anthology of Black American

Radical Abolition, Resistance, and Revolution

(1526 - 1865)

Written By: Anthony R. Stewart, Jr., JD.

ACKNOWLEDGMENTS

Dedicated to Morehouse College
— My intellectual and spiritual home—
the two for which I make no distinction.

Developmental Editor: Morgan A. Robinson,
Ph.D. Candidate
Spelman College; History, Bachelors
Georgetown University; International Studies;
Comparative History, Masters
Penn State; History and African American
Studies, Ph.D. Candidate

Line Editor: N'krumah Justice Colton

Cover Illustration: Dana J. Chandler
Master Artist

Academic Consultant: Darien Pollock, Ph.D.
Morehouse College; Philosophy, Bachelors
Harvard University; Philosophy. Ph.D.
Boston University; Assistant Professor of
Philosophy

ARSJ Media & Publishing House, LLC, January 2025

Library of Congress Cataloging-in-Publication Data
Stewart Jr., Anthony R, 2025—
By the Hand or by the Pen: An Anthology of Black American Radical Abolition, Resistance, and Revolution
(1526-1865)

Manufactured in the United States of America.

A WORD FROM THE AUTHOR

I find this to be necessary work that feeds my soul. May nary a coin nor promise of good fortune change my heart. I rue the day that I find it no longer fit to advocate for and preserve the history of my people. Most promisingly where it is deemed radical.

Author, Anthony R. Stewart, Jr., JD.

CONTENTS

The Hand

Drapetomania: (n.) The overwhelming urge of a slave to run away from his or her master. Coined as a mental disorder by physician Samuel Cartwright in 1851.

The San Miguel de Gualdape Slave Rebellion of 1526

The San Miguel de Gualdape Slave Rebellion of 1526 is one of the earliest recorded instances of enslaved Africans resisting their oppressors in the New World. The event occurred during a time when the transatlantic slave trade was just beginning to take root. This rebellion ignited in the Spanish colonial settlement of San Miguel de Gualdape, located in what is now the border of present-day Georgia and South Carolina.

San Miguel de Gualdape was part of Spain's early efforts to establish a foothold in North America following the successful Spanish colonization of parts of the Caribbean and South America. The settlement was established by Lucas Vázquez de Ayllón, a Spanish conquistador, and was the third settlement in North America north of present-day Mexico. The settlement was located near the Altamaha River, a region that had yet to be explored or settled by Europeans. The foreign settlers brought with them approximately one-hundred enslaved Africans from previous slave expeditions, marking the beginning of the transatlantic slave trade in what is now the United States.

Although the rebellion itself was relatively short-lived and not widely documented, it has remained an important event for understanding early slave resistance in the Americas, and the

1

harsh conditions that enslaved Africans faced in the colonies. The story of this uprising also reflects the fragile and chaotic nature of Spanish colonization in what was then deemed the "New World".

The settlement faced numerous challenges almost immediately. The land was swampy, the climate unfamiliar, and the indigenous population—the Guale tribe—were hostile and resistant to European encroachment. Additionally, the colony was located on the edge of Spanish influence and had little support from the Spanish crown, which led to instability from the outset. The Spanish settlers at San Miguel de Gualdape were isolated, with limited resources and no immediate prospect of reinforcements from Spain. The settlement struggled to sustain itself, and the colonists were fearful of attacks from the Indigenous peoples in the area. This sense of vulnerability and paranoia likely contributed to their mistreatment of the enslaved Africans, who were seen as property rather than people with their own rights and aspirations.

Among the enslaved people brought to San Miguel de Gualdape were a group of African captives from various tribes and ethnic backgrounds, who had been forcibly taken from West and Central Africa and brought to the Americas through the emerging slave trade. Their experiences would set the stage for a history of resistance against colonial and slaveholding systems in mainland America.

The enslaved people at San Miguel de Gualdape were subjected to brutal conditions,

2

working in agriculture and forced labor projects. They were considered property, bound to work for their Spanish masters under constant threat of punishment or death. The difficult living conditions, coupled with a sense of hopelessness, made life for the enslaved population unbearable. The settlement's harsh conditions—poor food quality, disease, inadequate shelter, and the grueling labor demanded of enslaved people— created a climate ripe for unrest. The Spanish crown was more focused on its colonies in the Caribbean and Central America and had little interest in supporting the struggling settlement of San Miguel de Gualdape. Life in the early colony was brutal for both the enslaved and the colonizers, but the enslaved people, who had no rights or autonomy, suffered most.

The rebellion at San Miguel de Gualdape was not an isolated event, but rather a culmination of aggravations and mistreatment by the hands of the Europeans. Ayllón died of dysentery and the settlement split into two factions. The first faction was taken over by Captain Francisco Gomez who wished to stay, and the other was claimed by Gines Doncel who wished to abandon the seemingly unsuccessful settlement. The lack of reinforcements, coupled with the colonists' inability to establish a sustainable economy or defend against local Indigenous groups, created a sense of frustration among settlers. While the two factions were at odds, several enslaved Africans set fire to many campsites, including the home of Doncel. While specific details of the rebellion are scarce, what is known is that in 1526, a group of enslaved

Africans revolted against their Spanish masters in a dramatic show of resistance.

According to some accounts, the enslaved Africans, motivated by their collective suffering and driven by the desire for freedom, launched a coordinated attack on their Spanish overseers. Armed with whatever weapons they could find, the enslaved rebels fought against the Spanish settlers and their guards in a desperate bid for freedom. Many fled to the jungles to live with isolated indigenous populations.

The history of African resistance to slavery in the New World had already begun to take shape in the Caribbean, where enslaved Africans had engaged in multiple revolts. Many of the Africans brought to San Miguel de Gualdape had likely witnessed or heard of uprisings in nearby regions and may have been inspired by these earlier acts of resistance. The enslaved Africans at San Miguel de Gualdape brought with them cultural and spiritual traditions that helped them resist their enslavement. African religions, music, language, and communal ties played a crucial role in forming a collective identity among the enslaved people, and these cultural bonds likely fostered a sense of solidarity in the face of oppression.

This act of resistance was significant for several reasons. First, it represented the first known act of large-scale rebellion by enslaved Africans in what would later become the United States. Second, it marked the beginning of a long history of enslaved people resisting oppression in the Americas, setting the stage for later, more

4

successful uprisings and the various slave rebellions in the Southern colonies. The failure of the San Miguel de Gualdape colony and the rebellion that preceded its collapse are often seen as a symbol of the difficulties Spain faced in establishing stable colonies in the New World. However, the story of the rebellion is also a testament to the resilience and resistance of the enslaved Africans who fought for their freedom in a world that sought to deny them their humanity.

The immediate aftermath of the rebellion saw the collapse of the San Miguel de Gualdape settlement. The colonists were unable to maintain control over the settlement due to the rebellion further weakening the already fragile community, and within a year of its establishment, San Miguel de Gualdape was abandoned. In 1527, the remaining settlers, along with a handful of recaptured Africans, left the site, ultimately heading to Hispaniola. The settlement was never resettled, and its location was soon lost to history, becoming an archaeological mystery for centuries. Out of the original 700 or so colonists who settled, only about 150 were left alive to make that voyage.

This event challenges the common narrative of enslaved Africans as passive victims, highlighting the agency and resistance of those who fought for their freedom in the face of overwhelming odds. The San Miguel de Gualdape Rebellion may have been forgotten by many, but it remains an important moment in the long history of Black resistance to enslavement and a powerful symbol of the enduring human spirit.

Gaspar Nyanga's Rebellion of 1570

The rebellion led by Gaspar Nyanga, an African leader of the Bran ethnic group belonging to a royal family in Gabon, was one of the earliest and most successful uprisings against Spanish colonial rule in the New World. His story, set in the rugged mountains of Veracruz, Mexico, and culminating in the 1570 rebellion, would become a beacon of hope for enslaved people across the Americas, showing that freedom was not a distant dream, but something that could be fought for, won, and sustained.

Gaspar Nyanga, often referred to as the "King of the Cimarrones" (runaways) was born around 1545, and like many Africans during this period, he was forcibly taken from his homeland and sold into the brutal system of slavery in the Spanish colonies. Nyanga's age at the time he was captured is unknown, but what is certain is that his spirit and leadership abilities were evident from a young age.

After being enslaved, Nyanga was transported to the Spanish colonial city of Veracruz, on the coast of modern-day Mexico. There he was forced to work on the sugar plantations that flourished in the area. Sugar and other cash crops were the cornerstone of Spanish colonial wealth, and the labor to produce these goods was extracted from the enslaved African and Indigenous peoples of that region. In this oppressive environment, the spark of rebellion began to grow in the hearts of those who were subjected to unimaginable cruelty.

6

It was during this time that Nyanga became a leader among the enslaved African workers. He and others eventually escaped from the Spanish plantations by force and sought refuge in the Sierra—the rugged mountain range near Veracruz. There, he founded a maroon community made up of African and Indigenous peoples who had escaped Spanish domination. These maroon societies, often located in the remote mountains situated near present day Córdoba, Mexico, became strongholds of resistance where runaways could live in relative freedom, evading Spanish patrols and organizing their own defense.

Nyanga's ability to unite different groups of people—enslaved Africans, Indigenous tribes, and even some of the marginalized poor—was a testament to his leadership. Over the years, his community in the mountains grew in both numbers and strength. Nyanga and his followers became known as cimarrones (runaways), and their mountain stronghold became an impenetrable fortress of resistance.

By the 1560s, Nyanga's maroon community had become a well-established base of rebellion. The Spanish, concerned with the growing number of escaped slaves and their rebellious activities, attempted several military expeditions to quell the cimarron threat, but they were unsuccessful. Nyanga's group was highly mobile, using the terrain to their advantage, and they were adept at ambushes and guerilla tactics. Nyanga's maroons ravaged the haciendas and farms within their reach to survive, by freeing slaves and killing Spaniards as they saw fit for

7

survival and success. Historical scholars believe that one of the community's most monumental accomplishments was their persistent attacks on the Viceroyalty-era Mexico-Veracruz Road, which connected the Gulf's main port with the capital of what was then considered New Spain. This road was one of the busiest transit and communication routes in the Americas and its economic prominence was essential for the development of New Spain. The Spanish authorities were frustrated by their inability to capture Nyanga or destroy his community, which was seen as a growing symbol of defiance to Spanish rule.

Despite the continuing raids and attempts by the Spanish to destroy his community, Nyanga's position was becoming increasingly confrontational. As the Spanish tightened their grip on the region, Nyanga realized that only a direct challenge to Spanish authority would secure his people's freedom. The most significant chapter in Nyanga's legacy came in 1570, when he decided to lead his people in an open rebellion against Spanish authority. The details of the revolt are unclear, but it is known that Nyanga, together with his forces, launched a daring offensive against Spanish forces in Veracruz. This rebellion was not just a desperate act; it was a well-coordinated and strategic assault that sought to challenge the very foundation of Spanish control in the region.

The Spanish response to Nyanga's rebellion was swift and harsh. The Spanish sent a large military force to capture him and destroy his community. However, they were met with fierce resistance. The guerilla tactics of Nyanga's

8

followers—combined with the advantage of fighting on their home turf in the mountains—made it nearly impossible for the Spanish to gain ground. The rebels had the knowledge of the land, which allowed them to strike swiftly and disappear into the terrain before the Spanish could retaliate.

Nyanga's rebellion of 1570 was not just about military confrontation. It was an act of symbolic defiance against the entire structure of Spanish colonialism. Nyanga and his followers demonstrated that they could resist the might of one of the world's most powerful empires, and for quite a time, they achieved their goal.

Despite their initial success in repelling the Spanish forces, Nyanga and his followers faced a difficult reality. While they had shown their military strength, they were outnumbered and lacked the resources to sustain a prolonged conflict. Rather than continue the struggle with the risk of being destroyed, Nyanga took a pragmatic approach that would become one of the defining moments of his leadership.

In 1571, after a year of intermittent conflict, Nyanga was able to negotiate a treaty with the Spanish crown. This was a remarkable achievement, as it was rare for enslaved people or rebellious communities to secure any kind of recognition from the Spanish authorities. The terms of the treaty allowed Nyanga and his followers to live in peace and freedom. The Spanish agreed to recognize their autonomy in exchange for a cessation of hostilities.

The terms of the treaty were as follows: (1) Nyanga and his followers were classified as free men and women and able to establish their own settlement in the mountains. They would be recognized as a "free town", and its people could live without fear of being attacker, captured and re-enslaved. (2) Rebels would no longer raid Spanish settlements.

This agreement effectively gave Nyanga's maroon community official recognition as free people, a rare and unprecedented concession from the Spanish. Nyanga had not only survived the conflict with Spain but had secured a victory for freedom. His rebellion and the resulting treaty were a powerful blow to the myth of Spanish invincibility in the Americas and set a precedent for other maroon communities to resist Spanish rule.

Gaspar Nyanga's victory in 1571 was a groundbreaking event in the history of resistance against slavery in the Americas. His success demonstrated that African enslaved people and their descendants could fight for their freedom and win. Nyanga's legacy is remembered in modern-day Mexico, where the town of "Nyanga", located in Veracruz, stands as a testament to his rebellion and leadership of over thirty years.

In 1932, the town of San Lorenzo de los Negros was renamed "Yanga" and was officially incorporated as a Mexican city. The Mexican government honored Nyanga by officially recognizing him as the first free black man in Mexico, and his legacy has since become an emblem of Afro-Mexican pride and resistance. His

10

community in the mountains, though small in number, became a symbol of what could be achieved through unity, strength, and an unyielding demand for freedom. Communities such as Yanga and other Black-Mexican towns served as safe havens for Black Americans in Texas, Arkansas, Alabama, and many other parts of the deep south that escaped to Mexico from the United States and found refuge.

Nyanga's rebellion of 1570 is one of the earliest and most significant examples of successful resistance against colonial oppression in the Western world, long before the great slave revolts of Haiti or the abolition movements that would sweep the Americas in the nineteenth century. His leadership reminds us that, while enslaved people are often viewed as powerless, they were capable of great acts of defiance and resistance—acts that would ultimately challenge and undo the systems of slavery that had held them captive for so long.

The Westmoreland Slave Conspiracy of 1687

The Westmoreland Slave Conspiracy of 1687 stands as one of the earliest and most significant moments of racial fear and repression in colonial America, reflecting the deep-seated anxieties about slavery, race, and the potential for Black resistance. The system of slavery was still taking root in the American colonies, and the economic and social structures of the time were built upon the labor of enslaved Africans. Yet, beneath this veneer of stability, there was an undercurrent of tension — a fear of insurrection from the enslaved who were forced into slavery, but who grew increasingly restless and discontented over time. The Westmoreland slave plot was the first conspiracy in British North America not involving the participation or support of poor, indentured Whites.

In the context of early Virginia, fears of a slave rebellion were constantly simmering. The Caribbean had witnessed several uprisings, and news of such revolts was known in the colonies. The idea that enslaved people might one day revolt against their oppressors was a constant source of anxiety for the White ruling class. These fears were not only rooted in the oppressive labor systems of slavery, but also in the racial and social order that had been carefully constructed to maintain the domination of White colonialists. The aftermath of the Westmoreland slave conspiracy left a lasting impact on how Virginia and other Southern colonies dealt with the

12

growing population of enslaved people and the fears that followed.

Three inter-racial conspiracies preceded the Westmoreland slave plot of 1687: (1) The York County Conspiracy of 1661; (2) The Gloucester County Conspiracy of 1663; and (3) Bacon's Rebellion of 1676, all of which included enslaved Africans and Indigenous peoples. It is likely that these events convinced the enslaved Africans of Virginia to work alone and exclude other groups who typically undermined them and used them as scapegoats when facing their European counterparts. For example, Nathaniel Bacon, of the latter conspiracy, killed many Indigenous and African people in the name of preserving the rights and futures of his own people against the British crown. European-American historians have long considered him a hero and the first true American Patriot.

Westmoreland County, located in the Northern neck of Virginia was a relatively affluent region of the colony—known for its tobacco plantations. In the 17th century, the majority of the region's workforce consisted of enslaved Africans who toiled in the tobacco fields under harsh conditions. They were treated as property, their every movement surveilled, and their rights non-existent. The system of slavery in Virginia was brutal, and although the enslaved were often forced to submit to their captors, there were instances of resistance and insurgence, which were suppressed with violent retribution.

13

By the 1680's, the enslaved population of Virginia had reached a critical mass. The origins of the 1687 slave plot can be traced to a growing sense of unrest among the enslaved population. As the tobacco economy grew, so did the number of African slaves in the colony. Those enslaved lived in a state of constant fear and deprivation, but they also harbored a sense of solidarity and an understanding of their collective power. Communication among slaves across plantations, especially in rural regions like Westmoreland, was a key factor in fomenting rebellion. The Virginia General Assembly passed an act in 1680 prohibiting the enslaved from carrying weapons, meeting in public, or travel without permission from a White man. The aftermath of the Westmoreland slave plot led to another act in 1690 being passed that allowed colonist to kill any slave who resisted, ran away, or refused to surrender when ordered.

The exact details of the 1687 Westmoreland slave plot are murky, but it is clear that the conspirators had a single goal: to overthrow their enslavers and seize control of the region. According to colonial records, the plot involved a small group of enslaved men and women who conspired to murder their masters, free themselves, and establish an independent community of runaways. They planned to strike at night, using surprise as their main advantage, and take the plantations by force

Despite the secrecy surrounding the plot, the conspiracy was discovered before it could come to fruition. On October 24, 1687, a panicked Nicholas Spencer provided

14

Virginia governor Francis Howard, with an account of a suspected slave conspiracy. Spencer, who lived in Westmoreland County, was himself a member of the Council as well as Secretary of State. According to the Council's journal, he provided "Intelligence of the discovery of a Negro Plot, formed in the Northern Neck for the destroying and killing of his Majesty's subjects the inhabitants thereof, with a design of Carrying it through the whole colony of Virginia ..."

The fate of the conspirators was grim. The accused slaves were executed by hanging or burnt alive in public displays meant to serve as warnings to any others who might consider rebelling. Colonial authorities ensured that the punishments were ruthless and highly visible to prevent other uprisings from following.

Although the 1687 plot was swiftly and violently suppressed, it was not an isolated incident. Throughout the 17th and 18th centuries, slave uprisings, conspiracies, and resistance movements continued to simmer beneath the surface of Virginia's plantation economy. The Westmoreland Slave Plot, though it ended in perceived failure, is significant in the broader history of slave resistance in the American colonies. It reflects the deep, abiding anger and frustration of an oppressed people who were determined to fight for their freedom, even in the face of overwhelming odds.

The Westmoreland plot also highlighted the tensions within Virginia's society—tensions that would continue to grow over the coming centuries. The loyalty of enslaved Africans to one another, their deep desire for freedom, and their willingness to resist oppression were themes that would resonate throughout the history of slavery in the United States. The plot was a precursor to larger, more famous uprisings, such as the 1712 New York slave rebellion and the 1831 Nat Turner rebellion, which demonstrated that the desire for freedom was a force that could not be easily extinguished.

One of the most frustrating aspects of the Westmoreland Slave Plot is the lack of detailed records. The names of the conspirators were never recorded, and the story is told through the lens of colonial authorities who sought to suppress any trace of rebellion. The voices of the enslaved individuals, who bore the brunt of the plot's consequences, are largely absent from historical accounts. Their motivations, emotions, and strategies remain mostly a mystery, leaving us to speculate about the lives of these brave men and women who sought to fight for their freedom.

In recent years, historians have started to re-examine slave rebellions and resistance movements from the perspective of the enslaved. While records of the Westmoreland Slave Plot are limited, scholars have used the available sources to piece together the events of the conspiracy, and in doing so, have shined a light on the broader context of slavery in Virginia and the ways in which enslaved Africans fought back against oppression.

The Westmoreland Slave Plot of 1687, though largely forgotten by mainstream history, represents a powerful symbol of the resistance that underpinned the African American experience during the colonial period. The echoes of rebellion in Westmoreland County remind us of the agency and resilience of enslaved people, whose fight for freedom, though often silenced, was an ongoing struggle that shaped the course of American history.

Slave Revolt of Newtown, Long Island, New York 1708

Slavery was the foundation of the socio-economic systems of the English colonies, and despite the relatively small population of African slaves in the northeastern colonies, the institution of slavery was just as malicious and dehumanizing as it was in the southern plantations. One of the more significant, though lesser-known, events of resistance to slavery in colonial New York occurred in 1708—the Slave Revolt of Newtown, Long Island—what is now known as Queens, New York.

The Slave Revolt of Newtown was one of the few documented slave uprisings in the northern colonies, which have often been overshadowed by the more notorious revolts of the South. However, it offers a poignant insight into the resilience of enslaved people, the deep-seated tensions in colonial society, and the precarious nature of colonial power dynamics.

Newtown, located on Long Island in the Province of New York, was a bustling town in the early 1700s. As a hub for trade, shipbuilding, and agriculture, the town had a relatively small but growing enslaved population. By the early 18th century, African slaves were increasingly working on farms, in households, and in emerging industries, contributing to the town's economic growth.

Slavery in Newtown was not as widespread as in the southern colonies, where large-scale

18

plantation agriculture demanded a sizeable, enslaved workforce. Instead, slaves in the northern colonies typically worked in domestic roles, small-scale farming, and trades such as blacksmithing, carpentry, and weaving. While some enslaved people had the opportunity to learn skilled trades, their lives were nonetheless defined by a lack of freedom, dignity, and autonomy.

By 1708, the tensions between enslaved people and their owners had reached a boiling point in Newtown. The violent conditions of their enslavement, coupled with the growing dissatisfaction among those denied basic rights, created a volatile environment for upheaval. The political and economic elites, who depended on slavery for their own prosperity, were keenly aware of the potential for resistance and the dangers of rebellion.

The events of the revolt began on a February 28, 1708. In the small, tightly knit community of Newtown, four enslaved persons decided they could no longer tolerate their condition. Driven by years of abuse, harsh working environments, and the trauma of separation from their families, one Black woman, Two Black Men, and one Black Indigenous hatched a plan to rebel.

Led by a charismatic and defiant enslaved man, whose name was undocumented, the revolt began with a covert gathering of enslaved individuals who plotted their rebellion in secret. One of the men, who was a skilled carpenter, had heard of similar uprisings in other parts of the

19

colonies and knew that rebellion was possible—even if the chances of success were slim. His message to the others was clear: "No longer will we serve in silence. The group, which included both men and women armed with tools, farm implements, and anything they could find to use as weapons, set ablaze the home of a slave owner. When the colonists rushed to extinguish the fire, they were ambushed by the rebels and heads were hatched. The rebels overwhelmed their masters in a burst of rage and vengeance. Those who had once been at the mercy of their master's now held the upper hand—if only for a moment.

The conspirators stormed the homes of the town's elite, killing some of their master's and injuring others. It was not just a revolt of desperation, but a demand for retribution—a claim to dignity, justice, and the right to live without fear of violence and humiliation. At least seven Whites were killed.

The authorities, upon hearing word of the revolt, quickly mobilized a response. The colonial militia was called into action, and troops began pouring into Newtown from nearby towns. It wasn't long before the enslaved rebels, many of whom had initially succeeded in taking over portions of the town, were cornered and overwhelmed by the superior firepower and coordination of the colonial forces.

The brutal crackdown was swift and merciless. Those who had been involved in the uprising were captured, and many African slaves were executed or punished severely—even those unaware that the plot existed. All four leaders of the revolt were apprehended after a few days of intense searching. The three enslaved men were executed by hanging, their bodies displayed as a grim reminder of the fate that awaited those who dared challenge the authority of the colonial elites. The brave and courageous lone woman was burned alive for all of Newtown's residents to see.

In total, several enslaved people were executed, while others were subjected to cruel punishment or returned to their masters maimed and in chains. The immediate aftermath of the revolt resulted in a tightening of restrictions on the enslaved population. Laws were passed by the New York Colonial Assembly to make it more difficult for slaves to organize and communicate, and the already strained relationship between enslaved Africans and their masters became even more oppressive.

The Slave Revolt of Newtown left an indelible mark on the collective memory of enslaved people in the region. Though the revolt was short-lived, it demonstrated that resistance, even in small and seemingly futile ways, was a persistent force in the colonies. It sent a clear message to the white elite that the enslaved population would not passively accept their bondage. The uprising also showed the colonial authorities that the enslaved were capable of organizing, planning, and executing a rebellion— even in the more temperate and seemingly less volatile northern colonies.

In the broader context of American slavery, the revolt of 1708 was part of a pattern of enslave opposition that spanned the entire colonial

21

period. From the violent uprisings in the Caribbean to the perceivably more subtle acts of defiance in the north, enslaved people continually sought to regain their humanity through small, often invisible forms of rebellion such as breaking tools and setting fire to the homes of enslavers.

Though the revolt was ultimately quelled, it contributed to a broader conversation in the colonies about slavery, resistance, and the limits of colonial authority. Enslaved people would continue to fight for their freedom in both open and subtle ways for the next several generations, with larger, more famous uprisings such as the Stono Rebellion of 1739 in South Carolina, the New York City slave conspiracy of 1741, and the eventual abolition of slavery in the United States.

The Slave Revolt of Newtown, Long Island in 1708 serves as a reminder of the constant tension between enslaved people and their masters in colonial America. It also highlights the often-overlooked history of resistance in the northern colonies. While the insurrection was brief and relatively unsuccessful, its legacy lives on in the broader history of African American resistance to slavery.

The New York Slave Rebellion of 1712

The New York Slave Rebellion of 1712 was a pivotal moment in the history of early Black American resistance to slavery. Despite being an isolated event, the rebellion provides insight into the depth of resistance among enslaved people, and the sadistic lengths to which colonial authorities went to maintain control. It stands as a testament to the strength and determination of the enslaved population in a time when slavery was an entrenched institution. The rebellion of 1712 highlights the racial and economic tensions that would continue to shape New York and the broader colonies for decades.

Enslaved Africans worked in various sectors, including agriculture, domestic labor, and as skilled artisans. The population of enslaved people in New York was smaller than that of southern colonies, such as Virginia and South Carolina, where slavery was the backbone of the economy. Despite this, New York had a large enough enslaved population to create constant racial and social tension.

The number of enslaved people in New York City and the surrounding areas grew over the late 17th and early 18th centuries, and by 1712, slaves comprised about one-fifth of the city's total population. They lived under terrible conditions, working long hours under the supervision of white masters and overseers, often in unfathomable and dehumanizing circumstances. Many were brought to New York from Africa

23

through the transatlantic slave trade or were born into slavery.

Despite the colony's reliance on enslaved labor, New York was also a city marked by cultural diversity. Alongside the European settlers, there were significant numbers of African slaves, Native Americans, and free Black people. The enslaved population, however, was subjected to increasingly rigid controls to maintain the social and economic order. Throughout the colony, fears of rebellion simmered beneath the surface, as enslaved Africans became more aware of their power and began to resist their inhumane treatment in various ways.

The New York Slave Rebellion of 1712 was not a spontaneous outburst, but rather the culmination of simmering tensions between the enslaved people and their oppressors. The rebellion began on the evening of April 6, 1712, when a group of enslaved Africans, many of whom had been brought to New York from different regions of Africa, organized an armed revolt against their masters.

The revolt began when a group of roughly 23 enslaved Africans, comprised of men and women, attacked their white overseers and masters. The ploy was meticulously planned: the rebels waited until nightfall before attacking a group of white men who were working in the city. They set fire to the buildings and launched a coordinated assault, killing over a dozen white people, including women and children. Several more were injured.

The revolt was not intended as an isolated attack; the enslaved people had hopes of rallying more rebels to their cause. They had planned to make their way to the nearby African community and to recruit other enslaved people, hoping to turn the rebellion into a widespread insurrection.

However, the insurgents were not able to fully execute their plan. Local white inhabitants, alerted by the fires and the violence, quickly mobilized to suppress the rebellion. The swift response by the local authorities overwhelmed the rebels. and the rebels were quickly overwhelmed. Within a few hours, most of the rebel leaders were either shot and killed or captured.

Robert Hunter, the colony's governor, immediately ordered the arrest of many of the suspected rebel conspirators. Many enslaved people, including those not involved in the revolt, were rounded up for interrogated and torture. The brutality of the repression that followed the rebellion served as a warning to any other enslaved people who might have been thinking of rebelling.

The captured rebels were put on trial: 27 enslaved people were executed or killed during the repression, many of them after being tortured. Some were burned alive, others hanged, while others were subjected to amputations or mutilations. The authorities made an example of the rebels to deter future uprisings. They would keep and give their children body parts, such as fingers, ears, or toes as souvenirs.

The public spectacle of these executions was meant to instill fear in the enslaved population, demonstrating the extreme lengths to which the authorities were willing to go to protect the status quo. As a result, the revolt had a chilling effect on any future attempts at resistance in the region. It also led to stricter laws governing the movement and behavior of enslaved people in the state of New York.

In the aftermath of the rebellion, the colonial government imposed new restrictions on enslaved persons. Gatherings, the ability to carry weapons, and t movement throughout the city were heavily surveillance. In many cases, enslaved people were required to be accompanied by a white person if they left their farm or work site. These laws aimed to prevent any future slave conspiracies or uprisings, and they reflected the growing fear among white colonists that slave rebellion was a real and present threat.

The 1712 uprising was one of the first major slave revolts in the Northern colonies to demonstrate that enslaved people could organize strong resistance campaigns. The courageous slaves involved showed that the institution of slavery, no matter how entrenched, would always be vulnerable to acts of defiance.

The New York Slave Rebellion of 1712 also served as an important precursor to later slave revolts in the United States, including the more famous New York City Uprising of 1741 and Nat Turner's Rebellion in 1831. It also highlighted the deep social and racial tensions within New York and the greater Atlantic world. The rebellion did

26

not result in the immediate liberation of enslaved individuals, but it did spark a conversation—albeit a provocative one—about the inherent injustice of slavery and the potential for collective resistance.

In telling the story of the 1712 New York Slave Rebellion, we honor the legacy of those who fought for freedom, and we recognize their place in the extensive struggle against the institution of slavery.

The Natchez Territory Uprising of 1730

The Natchez Uprising of 1730 is one of the most significant and tragic events in the history of colonial America, illustrating the explosive tensions between Indigenous peoples, African slaves, and European colonists. The uprising is a stark example of resistance, born of desperation, against brutal oppression. It also marks a pivotal moment in the collision of Native American sovereignty, the expansion of European settler colonialism, and the institution of slavery in the early Americas.

The Natchez people were a well-established and powerful Native American tribe living along the Mississippi River in present-day Mississippi and Louisiana. By the early 1700s, they were a thriving and independent society with a complex political structure, a rich spiritual tradition, and a strategic location. Their capital, the town of Natchez, was situated on a high bluff overlooking the river—a place of great cultural significance to the tribe.

In 1716, the French established Fort Rosalie near Natchez, a colonial outpost intended to protect French interests in the region. The French were keen to expand their empire in North America and, to that end, sought to gain control of the Natchez people and the surrounding lands. In doing so, they began to impose colonial structures of power over the Native populations, including demanding labor, establishing trade monopolies, and controlling land distribution.

28

The French colonists, though initially eager to establish peaceful trade relations with the Natchez, were increasingly drawn into the exploitative practices of settler colonialism.

At Fort Rosalie, the French quickly established a system of slavery, bringing enslaved Africans to work the fields, particularly in tobacco and indigo cultivation. The enslaved Africans, though isolated from the larger Atlantic slave trade at first, faced horrific conditions under the French colonists. The French settlers utilized both coercion and violence to maintain control over the African slaves and the Native populations, fostering growing discontent on both fronts.

By 1729, tension between the Natchez people and the French had reached a breaking point. Several factors contributed to the eventual uprising, among which were:

Brutal Treatment of the Natchez People: The French were increasingly encroaching upon Natchez lands, appropriating resources and demanding tribute from the local tribes. The French authorities were dismissive of Native sovereignty, and the abuse of power was a persistent source of grievance. French commanders at Fort Rosalie had taken aggressive steps to suppress the Natchez's independence, including forcing the tribe to provide labor for the construction of fortifications, and seizing land for plantations and other colonial ventures.

The Expansion of Slavery: The French brought African slaves to Fort Rosalie in increasing numbers, exacerbating existing racial and cultural tensions. While the Natchez were initially hesitant to take enslaved Africans into their midst, the settlers sought to use slavery as a tool to weaken the Natchez. To the Natchez, the presence of enslaved people was an affront to their freedom and autonomy, as well as a reminder of the broader power dynamics in play. The enslaved Africans, for their part, often empathized with the plight of the Native peoples, forming bonds of solidarity that would later prove crucial in the uprising.

Religious and Cultural Confrontations: French colonists, particularly Catholic missionaries, attempted to convert the Natchez to Christianity. These efforts were seen by the Natchez as an attack on their religious and cultural identity, as the French sought to erase or marginalize the Natchez's own belief systems. The imposition of Christianity and the disregard for Natchez traditions further alienated the tribe from the colonists.

Economic Exploitation: The French in the region were focused on trade and the cultivation of cash crops such as tobacco and indigo. For the Natchez, this meant losing control of their land and resources, which had once been abundant. The French, through trade monopolies and military power, sought to exploit the natural wealth of the region without regard for the wellbeing of the Natchez people.

On November 29, 1729, a carefully planned revolt erupted. The Natchez people and enslaved Africans who toiled for the French, led by tribal leaders, attacked Fort Rosalie with brutal force. The uprising, which would later be known as the Natchez Uprising, was not simply a reaction to the oppressive conditions imposed by the French, but also a rejection of the broader colonial system. The Natchez attacked French settlers viciously and persistently.

The first wave of the attack was swift and devastating. The Natchez forces, numbering some 300 warriors, struck in the early morning, catching the French off guard. They killed nearly 230 French settlers— men, women, and children—and destroyed much of Fort Rosalie. The French garrison at the fort was decimated, and the enslaved Africans—many of whom had been forced to work on the fortifications—joined in the rebellion, seizing the opportunity to escape their bondage.

As the Natchez warriors advanced, they also took control of the surrounding plantations and settlements. The uprising quickly spread beyond Fort Rosalie, as other Indigenous groups in the area joined the rebellion. The goal was to eliminate French colonial power in the region and establish a new order—one where the Natchez and their African allies could live freely without the threat of settler encroachment.

In response to the uprising, the French mobilized a counterattack. The French governor of Louisiana, Jean-Baptiste Le Moyne de Bienville, sent an army to crush the rebellion, and they were joined by a number of allied Native tribes, including the Choctaw. The French retaliated with unparalleled violence, using

31

military force to suppress the Natchez and any allies they had. The French destroyed Natchez villages and pursued fleeing survivors.

The French also captured a number of Natchez people, subjecting them to brutal punishment. Many were executed or sold into slavery in the Caribbean, where they would face even harsher conditions. The remnants of the Natchez tribe were forced to flee, with many seeking refuge among other tribes or in Spanish-controlled territories to the west.

The French also executed several enslaved Africans who had participated in the rebellion, sending a clear message about the lengths to which they would go to preserve the institution of slavery. Despite their brutal response, the French were never able to eliminate the threat posed by the Natchez and other tribes. The uprising marked the beginning of the end of French colonial power in the Mississippi Valley, as French control over the region steadily diminished following the attack.

The Natchez Uprising of 1730 remains an important historical moment for several reasons. It was one of the earliest large-scale uprisings against colonial authority in the Mississippi Valley, and it revealed the profound tensions between Indigenous peoples, enslaved Africans, and European settlers. The rebellion highlighted the possibility of cross-racial alliances between enslaved Africans and Native peoples in resistance to European colonial powers. It also demonstrated the lengths to which colonized people—both Indigenous and African—would go to assert their sovereignty and seek freedom from tyranny.

The Natchez Uprising was not an isolated incident; it was part of a broader pattern of resistance across the Americas. As slavery spread across the continent, resistance also grew, and uprisings such as the Natchez revolt contributed to the broader context of the fight for freedom that would define the history of the Americas.

In the aftermath, the Natchez were scattered and weakened, but their defiance left a lasting impression. Their rebellion, although crushed, was a profound assertion of their agency in a time when Indigenous peoples were being systematically marginalized and displaced. The Natchez, like many other Native tribes, would continue to resist colonialism, but the 1730 uprising remains a crucial chapter in their struggle for autonomy and justice.

The Natchez Uprising of 1730 serves as both a powerful symbol of resistance and a tragic reminder of the violence and exploitation that defined the colonial period in the Americas. It represents the struggle of oppressed peoples— Native and African alike—who, in the face of brutal repression, fought to assert their freedom. Though the uprising was ultimately crushed by the French, its legacy lived on as an example of resistance that would inspire generations to come.

The Stono Rebellion of 1739.

The Stono Rebellion, which took place on September 9, 1739, in the colony of South Carolina, is one of the most successful slave revolts in American history. Involving around 20 enslaved Africans who were primarily from the Congo region, the uprising would become the deadliest and largest slave rebellion in the colonies prior to the American Revolution. This event marked a turning point in the history of slavery in the American South, sparking a wave of fear and repression among slaveholders and forcing significant changes in slave laws and control tactics.

The Stono Rebellion not only illuminated the twisted realities of slavery but also demonstrated the lengths to which enslaved people would go to fight for their freedom. It also served as a grim reminder to colonial authorities of the dangers posed by a large, enslaved population and the potential for insurrection. In the wake of the rebellion, both the South Carolina government and plantation owners enacted stricter laws to prevent further uprisings.

This chapter explores the causes of the Stono Rebellion, the events that transpired, the aftermath, and its enduring legacy in the struggle for freedom and the fight against slavery.

In the early 18th century, South Carolina was one of the wealthiest and most slave-dependent colonies in the American South. The plantation economy, centered around the cultivation of rice and indigo, relied heavily on the labor of enslaved Africans, who made up a significant portion of the population. By 1739, enslaved Africans outnumbered white settlers in the colony by a ratio of about two to one.

Most of the enslaved people in South Carolina were from West and Central Africa, with large numbers coming from the region that is now Angola and the Congo. These Africans brought with them a rich cultural heritage, including spiritual beliefs, language, and traditions, which became a source of solidarity and resistance against the institution of slavery.

The enslaved people on South Carolina's plantations were subjected to brutal working conditions. They worked long hours in the rice fields, performing back-breaking labor under the constant threat of physical punishment. The laws governing slavery in South Carolina were designed to control every aspect of the lives of enslaved people, severely limiting their autonomy, mobility, and ability to communicate with one another.

Despite these harsh conditions, the enslaved Africans resisted their oppression in various ways, from day-to-day acts of defiance such as slowing down work or feigning illness to more overt forms of resistance, including running away and, in rare cases, outright rebellion. In this environment, the seeds of the Stono Rebellion were planted.

One of the key factors contributing to the rebellion was the growing unrest among the enslaved population, driven by a combination of oppressive conditions and the desire for freedom. In particular, the Angolan-born Africans were known to have a history of resistance to slavery, which included previous uprisings in the colonies and a deep cultural resistance against European colonial rule. The colony of South Carolina, in particular, had been a target of various slave conspiracies and smaller uprisings.

Additionally, news of slave rebellions in other parts of the Americas—especially the Cuban slave revolt of 1733—had spread to the South Carolina colony, fueling hopes for an African-led insurrection. This global context of slave resistance is vital to understanding the motivation behind the Stono Rebellion.

The Stono Rebellion began on the morning of September 9, 1739, near the Stono River, about 20 miles southwest of Charleston. A group of enslaved Africans, led by an individual named Jemmy, who was likely from the Kingdom of Kongo in present day Angola, began their march toward freedom. Jemmy and his followers, armed with guns and other weapons, first attacked a store house, killing two white men and stealing additional firearms, ammunition, and supplies. They then set fire to the store and began their march, rallying other enslaved Africans along the way.

The rebels, who had been planning the revolt for weeks, moved swiftly through the countryside, recruiting additional enslaved people to join their cause. They shouted "Liberty!" as they marched, signaling that their aim was not

36

just to escape but to fight for freedom. They made their way toward the Spanish-controlled Florida, where Spanish authorities had promised freedom to enslaved people who escaped from British colonies, further encouraging the rebels. These Floridians were believed to be kinsmen of the Black Seminoles

As they traveled, the group grew to around 60 to 100 rebels. They attacked plantations along the way, killing at least 30 white people. The rebels displayed a high level of coordination, and the violence was brutal—plantation owners and their families were killed indiscriminately. The enslaved people who joined the rebellion took weapons and supplies from the plantations, setting fire to the homes and fields of their oppressors. It was a desperate and bloody attempt to break free from the brutal system of slavery.

The rebellion did not go unnoticed. News of the uprising quickly spread to the nearby settlements, and a group of white militia forces was assembled to pursue the rebels. The militias were made up of local white colonists and Native American allies who were loyal to the colonial authorities.

Despite their initial success, the rebels were eventually caught by the militia. After several days of fighting, the rebellion was overcome near the Edisto River. Many of the insurgents were killed in battle or executed afterward. Jemmy, the leader of the revolt, was killed, and several of his fellow rebels were captured and publicly executed. In total, between

60 and 100 people were killed, with most of them being enslaved Africans.

The Stono Rebellion sent shockwaves through the South Carolina colony and the larger British colonial world. White slaveholders were terrified by the bloodshed and the prospect of future uprisings. In response, the South Carolina government enacted The Negro Act of 1740, one of the most repressive pieces of legislation aimed at controlling enslaved people. The act restricted the movement of enslaved Africans, forbade them from assembling in groups of more than three, and banned them from learning to read and write, often punished by death.

The rebellion also sparked a tightening of existing laws governing enslaved people, with more severe punishments for those caught attempting to escape or engage in acts of rebellion. The fear of further insurrection led to a greater militarization of slave patrols, and the presence of armed guards on plantations became more common. Plantation owners began to take even greater precautions, placing stricter controls over the lives of their enslaved workers.

While the rebellion was ultimately subdued, the legacy of the Stono Rebellion endured. It remained a symbol of Black resistance to slavery, inspiring future generations of enslaved people and abolitionists alike. The rebellion highlighted the deep divisions between the enslaved and their masters, and it revealed the potential for violence and insurrection that lay beneath the surface of the slave economy.

The Stono Rebellion, though short-lived, had lasting implications for both the institution of slavery and the broader struggle for freedom in America. It demonstrated the lengths to which enslaved people would go to secure their freedom, even in the face of extreme oppression and danger. It also revealed the vulnerability of the slave system, showing that, despite the systemic control and violence directed at them, enslaved people would resist in any way they could.

In the years following the Stono Rebellion, other slave uprisings and acts of resistance continued to shape the history of slavery in the United States, from smaller conspiracies to larger revolts like the Gabriel Prosser Rebellion in 1800. The fear of rebellion would remain a constant for slaveholders, and it would continue to influence policies surrounding slavery and control throughout the antebellum period.

Today, the Stono Rebellion is remembered as a critical moment in the history of slavery and African American resistance. It is a testament to the resilience of those who fought for freedom, even in the face of overwhelming odds. The Stono Rebellion is not just a historical event but a symbol of the enduring struggle for liberty, justice, and human dignity.

The New York Conspiracy of 1741

In a city where approximately 1,700 Black residents lived alongside 7,000 White inhabitants, tensions between the two groups were bound to erupt. With a system of slavery that sought to dehumanize every person of African descent, the potential for rebellion seemed inevitable. In early 1741, the unrest began when Fort George, a central military post in New York, was destroyed by fire. In the following weeks, fires broke out across the city— four in a single day—spreading to areas in New Jersey and Long Island. Rumors quickly circulated that enslaved Black people had boasted of starting the fires and threatened even greater violence.

Many Whites came to believe that these fires were part of a well-coordinated revolt orchestrated by secret Black societies and rebellious gangs. They imagined a vast conspiracy, one that involved not just enslaved people but free Blacks, poor Whites, and even Catholic priests—some with foreign connections to Black populations in the Caribbean. The narrative of a conspiracy took hold, especially among those who feared that a racial uprising could unravel their grip on power.

Ethnic and cultural groups that could have plausibly been seen as leaders of such resistance were identified by the authorities, including the Papa people from the Slave Coast in present-day Benin, the Igbo from the Niger River region, and the Malagasy from Madagascar. One particularly

40

suspicious group of slaves were the so-called "Cuba People"—enslaved Black people and mulattoes who had been captured in Cuba in the spring of 1740. These individuals had likely arrived in New York from Havana, the largest port in the Spanish West Indies, where there existed a significant free Black population. For these formerly free people, their sudden enslavement in New York was a bitter injustice, fostering resentment that may have been perceived as part of a larger plot.

The fear of an impending uprising was fueled further by the testimony of a 16-year-old Irish indentured servant. Arrested for theft, the young man claimed knowledge of a plot in which enslaved people, along with a few White conspirators, were planning to kill White men, capture White women, and set fire to the city. This confession, made under duress, triggered a wave of arrests and investigations.

In the end, 30 Black men, 2 White men, and 2 White women were executed for their alleged involvement in the conspiracy. 70 people of African descent were exiled to remote destinations like Newfoundland, Madeira, Saint-Domingue (which would later become Haiti), and Curaçao. Before the summer of 1741 ended, 17 Black men had been hanged, and 13 more were burned at the stake, becoming grotesque symbols of White fears fueled by the institution of slavery that they desperately sought to preserve.

The Great Negro Plot of 1741 serves as a stark reminder of how easily fear and racial paranoia can lead to collective hysteria, false

41

accusations, and a tragic loss of life. The conspiracy, whether real or fabricated, exposed the profound divisions in colonial New York and underscored the brutal measures that would be taken to preserve the status quo of Whiteness. In the end, it was not only the individuals accused of conspiracy who suffered; the very foundations of the system of slavery were shown to rest on an endless cycle of fear and violence that didn't care who was punished so long as punishment was administered.

Slaves on William Dunbar's Plantation Plan to Revolt 1776

The year of 1776 saw one of the most significant and little-known slave conspiracies in the history of colonial Louisiana. On the plantation of William Dunbar, a wealthy British-born plantation owner, a group of enslaved Africans were discovered plotting an uprising that would have had profound consequences for both their oppressors and the nascent colonial society.

William Dunbar was a prominent figure in colonial Louisiana. Originally from Scotland, Dunbar had come to the Mississippi River region in the mid-18th century and established a successful plantation along the banks of the Mississippi River near present-day New Orleans. As an influential landowner and a member of the colonial elite, Dunbar's wealth was rooted in the cultivation of indigo and tobacco, which were labor-intensive crops that required a large, enslaved workforce to sustain.

Like many plantation owners in Louisiana, Dunbar relied heavily on enslaved people to work his fields, and his estate became home to a significant number of enslaved Africans. These individuals, who had been forcibly brought to Louisiana from various parts of Africa, were subjected to the grueling, dehumanizing conditions that defined the plantation system. Life on Dunbar's plantation, like most others, was marked by long hours of hard labor, cruel punishment for perceived disobedience, and limited hope for freedom.

43

By the 1770s, the social and political atmosphere in Louisiana was becoming more complex. The region was a melting pot of French, Spanish, African, and Native American cultures, with slavery deeply entrenched in the economic system. Enslaved people, especially in the larger plantations along the Mississippi River, often lived in close quarters, bound together by shared experiences of oppression. Over time, this fostered a sense of community and solidarity, which would become vital to the conspiracy that unfolded in 1776.

In 1776, the enslaved people on Dunbar's plantation were suffering under the harsh conditions. Tensions were high, as rumors of a broader unrest among the enslaved population had begun to circulate throughout Louisiana. Enslaved people, many of whom had come from different parts of Africa, brought with them various forms of resistance—whether through small acts of defiance, work slowdowns, or subtle sabotage. But the conspiracy on Dunbar's plantation was an organized, deliberate plot to overthrow their oppressors and seek their freedom.

The conspiracy was organized by a group of enslaved men and women who had long discussed the possibility of rebellion. The group's leaders were skilled in secretive communications, likely using a network of covert signals and clandestine meetings to plan the revolt. At its core, the conspiracy sought to seize control of Dunbar's plantation, kill or overpower the overseers and white plantation owners, and escape to the freedom that many believed lay

44

beyond the reach of their captors. They also sought to rally other enslaved people in the region to their cause, hoping to spark a larger insurrection that could spread across the Louisiana territory.

The conspirators knew that the odds were against them. They had seen the punishment meted out to enslaved people who tried to escape or rebel, and they were aware of the harsh retaliation that would likely follow any uprising. However, the desire for freedom and the hope that they might join a broader movement for liberty gave them the courage to take the risk. They planned to strike when the plantation's overseers and other white residents were least expecting it—perhaps in the dead of night, when they would have the element of surprise on their side.

Unfortunately for the conspirators, their plan was discovered before it could be executed. The details surrounding the betrayal are unclear, but it is believed that a few members of the conspiracy had second thoughts and alerted the plantation's overseers. The network of enslaved people involved in the plot was infiltrated, and the conspiracy was uncovered. Historically, most rebellions and acts of defiance were quelled because of spineless slaves who squealed due to fear or hopes that they would be in the master's good favor.

When the plot was discovered, the French colonial authorities, who had control over Louisiana at the time, reacted swiftly and decisively. They were determined to prevent any threat to the established social order. The

45

conspirators were arrested, and the authorities moved quickly to suppress any potential for future unrest.

The captured conspirators were subjected to violent interrogations and faced brutal retribution. While many of those involved in the plot were executed—either hanged or burned at the stake—others were sent to the infamous Spanish-controlled Louisiana prison system, where they would be forced to endure hard labor and severe punishment for the rest of their lives. As if that wasn't already their fate.

The failed rebellion of 1776 sent shockwaves through the ranks of the enslaved population, as well as through the colonial authorities. The French and Spanish rulers of Louisiana were deeply concerned about the potential for further unrest, especially as the 18th century was marked by a series of slave revolts throughout the Americas, many which would begin later that decade. To prevent further insurrections, the French colonial government imposed even stricter regulations on enslaved people.

The consequences for the plotters and their families were severe. The repression following the discovery of the conspiracy extended beyond the immediate individuals involved, as colonial authorities feared the potential for future uprisings. Enslaved people were subjected to more intense surveillance, and harsh punishment was meted out not only to the leaders of the conspiracy but also to any individuals suspected of harboring rebellious thoughts or of encouraging resistance.

The plot's failure was a significant blow to the hopes of enslaved people on Dunbar's plantation and in the surrounding areas. However, it did not quell the spirit of resistance entirely. In fact, the plot's discovery and the brutal crackdown served to fuel resentment and mistrust between enslaved people and their masters, further cementing the understanding among the enslaved that their freedom could only be won by taking it.

Although the rebellion on William Dunbar's plantation was short-lived, its significance cannot be overstated. It was one of many instances of enslaved resistance in colonial America that highlighted the persistence of the desire for freedom among enslaved Africans and African Americans. These revolts, while often crushed, helped lay the foundation for the broader history of resistance that would culminate in the abolition of slavery.

In the larger context of the Revolutionary War, the conspiracy also foreshadowed the ways in which enslaved people would align themselves with both sides of the conflict. Many enslaved people, especially those in Louisiana, would later join the ranks of the British, who promised freedom to enslaved people who fled their colonial masters. Others sided with the American revolutionaries, hoping that independence from Britain might lead to their own emancipation.

The 1776 slave conspiracy on Dunbar's plantation is a reminder of the deep undercurrent of rebellion that ran through the institution of slavery. It reveals the extent to which enslaved people in colonial Louisiana were willing to risk their lives for a chance at freedom and the lengths to which they would go to resist their oppression. Though the plot was foiled by whistleblowers, the courage and resilience of those involved continue to serve as a testament to the indomitable spirit of resistance that would echo through the centuries in the fight for freedom.

Ona Judge: The Woman Who Escaped the First President 1796

Ona Judge's story is one of courage, perseverance, and resistance—a powerful reminder of the lengths to which enslaved people would go to reclaim their freedom. Her escape from the household of George and Martha Washington in the early 19th century is not just a personal act of defiance against the institution of slavery, but a historical moment that underscores the complex relationship between the first President of the United States and the system of enslavement that underpinned his wealth and power.

Ona Judge's escape, and the years she spent on the run afterward, may have been overshadowed by the famed narratives of U.S. history, but her legacy is crucial to understanding the deep contradictions at the heart of the American Revolution and the fight for freedom. She defied not only the physical and institutional systems of slavery but also the deeply ingrained social hierarchies that sought to keep her in bondage.

Ona Maria Judge was born around 1773, likely in the years just after the American Revolution, in the colonial estate of Mount Vernon, Virginia. She was the daughter of an enslaved woman named Betty, who was also held by George Washington. Ona was part of many enslaved people who worked at Mount Vernon, which was both a plantation and the Washington family's personal residence. George Washington,

49

the first President of the United States, owned more than 100 enslaved individuals during his lifetime.

From an early age, Ona worked in the kitchens and laundry rooms at Mount Vernon, learning domestic skills that would make her an important member of the Washington household. Her life was one of forced labor, with little to no agency over her own choices or future. The enslaved people at Mount Vernon, including Ona, were subject to harsh working conditions and the threat of being sold or moved to another plantation, breaking families apart. Despite these harsh realities, Ona's story was unique because of the privilege she briefly held as a personal servant to Martha Washington.

In the early 1790s, when George Washington became President, Ona Judge was brought to Philadelphia with Martha Washington. At the time, Pennsylvania had passed the Gradual Abolition Act of 1780, which required that enslaved individuals who lived in the state for more than six months be granted freedom. The Washingtons were aware of this law, and their solution was to rotate their enslaved people in and out of the state, thus ensuring they were never in Pennsylvania for long enough to gain their freedom.

Ona was brought to Philadelphia as part of Martha Washington's household staff. At first, Ona's role was relatively minor, though she worked closely with Martha and other members of the first family. As time went on, however, Ona became more involved in the personal service of the Washingtons, working as Martha's personal attendant.

This move to Philadelphia proved to be the critical turning point in Ona's life. While living in the city, Ona began to understand that she was living in a place where enslaved people had a path to freedom. She also became increasingly aware of the contradictions in the lives of the Washingtons—the ideals of liberty and freedom that they espoused as part of the new nation's foundation, contrasted sharply with the reality of their ownership of enslaved people.

Ona Judge's decision to escape slavery was driven by her longing for freedom and her growing realization that she had the legal right to claim it. In 1796, Ona learned that Martha Washington intended to free her as a wedding gift to her granddaughter, Elizabeth Parke Custis. This information changed Ona's perception of her future—she was not going to be freed immediately, and it became clear that the Washingtons had no intention of letting her go anytime soon.

Ona, now in her mid-20s, began to plan her escape. She knew the risks involved—if caught, she could be severely punished, and the Washingtons would certainly spare no effort to bring her back. But Ona was determined. She began to quietly gather information about Philadelphia's legal protections for free Black people, reaching out to local abolitionists and free Black communities who might help her.

In May 1796, Ona took advantage of a moment when Martha Washington was busy with other matters. With little more than the clothes on her back and the will to live freely, Ona escaped the Washington household. She fled the Washingtons' home, leaving behind her family and the security of her position, and sought refuge in the city's growing free Black population.

Philadelphia at the time had a large community of free Black people and abolitionists, and Ona sought their help. She also made contact with a local tailor named James Forten, a wealthy and influential Black man who became one of her most trusted allies in her pursuit of freedom.

After Ona's escape, the Washingtons were determined to bring her back. George Washington, who had long prided himself on his authority, was deeply offended by Ona's flight. He wrote letters to local officials and even attempted to bribe those who might have knowledge of her whereabouts. Washington's legal team used every tool at their disposal to track her down, offering large rewards for her capture and return. However, despite their efforts, Ona was able to evade them for the entirety of their pursuit.

For years, the Washingtons' frustration grew. In their eyes, Ona's escape was an insult not just to them personally, but also to the system of slavery that upheld their wealth and social status. Yet, despite the efforts of the Washingtons to recapture her, Ona remained hidden in the free Black communities of Philadelphia and later in New Hampshire, where she lived under the protection of abolitionists.

Ona Judge's escape was successful, but her life as a free woman was not without its challenges. She initially lived in Philadelphia, where she worked as a seamstress, and later moved to New Hampshire, where she found more permanent refuge. There, Ona married a free Black man named Jack Staines, with whom she had three children. Throughout her years in the North, Ona faced the constant threat of being captured and returned to slavery, as laws like the Fugitive Slave Act of 1793 allowed enslavers to reclaim runaway slaves even in free states.

Despite these constant threats, Ona lived the rest of her life as a free woman. In interviews conducted later in her life, Ona spoke about her pride in her decision to escape and the pain of having left behind her family. She expressed gratitude for the people who helped her during her time in hiding and in the pursuit of freedom.

Ona Judge's story is a powerful example of an individual's fight for freedom in a world built on the exploitation of Black people. She was not a passive figure in her own life. In fleeing the Washington household, she was not simply escaping one plantation—she was defying the very foundations of a nation that prided itself on liberty while holding millions of people in bondage.

Her escape also serves as a stark reminder of the hypocrisy embedded in the fabric of the United States. George Washington, the "Father of the Nation," who fought for freedom and independence, was himself a slave owner, as were many of the nation's founders. Ona Judge's

53

escape from his household is a challenge to the myth of benevolent slaveholding and a call to acknowledge the enslaved people who built this nation without recognition or reward.

Ona Judge's story is also a story of resilience. She spent decades living in fear of being caught, but she remained steadfast in her commitment to freedom, never losing sight of her dignity and humanity. Despite being pursued by one of the most powerful families in the United States, she outwitted them and lived out her life as a free woman.

Today, Ona Judge's legacy serves as a reminder of the countless enslaved people who fought not just for physical freedom, but for the right to live their lives according to their own will. Her life stands as a testament to the power of defiance in the face of systemic oppression and the enduring strength of the human spirit.

Hercules: Enslaved by the Washington Household 1797

Hercules, a skilled chef enslaved by George Washington, is often remembered as one of the most significant yet overlooked figures in the fight for freedom in early America. His escape from Mount Vernon, Washington's estate, is a tale of daring defiance—a story of one man's quest for liberty, despite the heavy chains of enslavement. His life is an exploration of the contradictions inherent in the newly formed United States, a nation that prided itself on the ideals of freedom and democracy, while simultaneously upholding the brutal institution of slavery.

Though Hercules's life and escape have been largely overshadowed by other figures in American history, his story is an essential chapter in the broader narrative of resistance against slavery and the courageous actions of enslaved people seeking freedom.

Hercules was born around 1754, likely in the early years of George Washington's time as a Virginia landowner. Hercules was initially enslaved by the Fairfax family, another wealthy plantation-owning family in Virginia, before being sent to George Washington's Mount Vernon estate as a young man. As a talented and ambitious cook, Hercules's skills were quickly recognized, and he became an integral part of Washington's household. In a system where most enslaved individuals worked in the fields or performed menial labor, Hercules's position as

55

head chef in Washington's kitchen was one of relative privilege.

Mount Vernon, Washington's sprawling estate along the Potomac River, was not just a plantation—it was also the site of political and social gatherings, a place where Washington hosted foreign dignitaries, high-ranking military officials, and influential figures of the new republic. The role of head chef was no small matter, and Hercules's talents were central to the estate's reputation. He prepared elaborate meals for Washington and his guests, including French-inspired dishes that elevated Mount Vernon's status. It is said that he cooked for many dignitaries, including Thomas Jefferson and the Marquis de Lafayette, who came to visit Washington during the Revolutionary War.

Despite the privileged nature of his position, Hercules was still enslaved, still subject to the whims of his master, and still a man denied his basic human rights. His skill in the kitchen did not protect him from the brutal system of slavery. As an enslaved man, Hercules lived with the constant threat of being sold away from his family or being subjected to harsher labor on the fields. His elevated position did little to shield him from the systemic violence of enslavement.

The irony of Hercules's situation was not lost on him. While he cooked meals that embodied the ideals of French refinement and wealth, he lived a life of deprivation. He was aware of the contradictions that lay at the heart of the Washingtons' existence—men who fought for liberty and independence while owning human beings who were denied their freedom. As George Washington became more entangled in his political career, Hercules may have become increasingly aware that freedom was not meant for him within the framework of Mount Vernon and the society that Washington upheld.

The hypocrisy was evident: Washington, one of the key figures in the American Revolution, believed in liberty for all, yet he held hundreds of enslaved people in bondage. Hercules may have heard Washington speak of the ideals of freedom and democracy, yet his own life under the master's roof was governed by the brutal realities of slavery. Washington's failure to free the people he enslaved—despite his public advocacy for liberty—would have been a daily reminder of the deep injustice inherent in the new nation.

By 1796, Hercules had lived and worked at Mount Vernon for more than 30 years. While his skill in the kitchen had earned him a certain level of importance, it did not guarantee him the freedom he so desperately sought. Hercules's longing for freedom would have intensified, especially as he learned that Washington had no intention of freeing him anytime soon. Washington had, at times, freed some of his enslaved people upon their deaths or after years of service, but Hercules, like many others, remained bound by the institution of slavery.

In 1796, Hercules made a fateful decision that would change the course of his life: he would escape. With his knowledge of Mount Vernon's layout and the connections he had made over the years, he carefully plotted his departure. The

57

risks were immense—if he were caught, he would face severe punishment or even death. But Hercules had spent much of his life under the yoke of enslavement, and the hope of freedom outweighed the fear of retribution.

The details of his escape are somewhat murky, but it is believed that Hercules managed to flee Mount Vernon by taking advantage of his position and the routine of Washington's household. As head chef, he likely had some autonomy and movement around the estate, which he could exploit to slip away undetected. It is possible that he received help from others at Mount Vernon or in the surrounding area, as enslaved people often relied on networks of solidarity and support from abolitionists and free Black communities.

Hercules's escape likely took him to Philadelphia, where many enslaved people sought refuge due to Pennsylvania's Gradual Abolition Act of 1780, which allowed enslaved individuals to claim freedom after living in the state for six months. Philadelphia was also home to a growing network of free Black people and abolitionists who worked together to protect runaways like Hercules. It was there that Hercules could find his footing as a free man—at least, for a time.

Once Hercules fled, George Washington was determined to bring him back. Hercules had been a valuable servant for years, and his escape was a personal affront to Washington. Washington was deeply troubled by the flight of his trusted chef and took immediate action to capture him. He sent agents and wrote letters to local officials, offering rewards for information that could lead to Hercules's capture. For the Washingtons, the defection of their slave was not merely a matter of lost labor—it was an attack on the order they sought to maintain.

Despite the efforts of Washington and his agents, Hercules evaded capture. The fugitive slave laws of the time allowed enslavers to pursue and retrieve runaways in any state, but Hercules used his knowledge of the terrain and the support of Philadelphia's Black community to stay hidden. Hercules was not alone in his flight—he was part of a broader resistance movement that saw enslaved people not only fighting for their freedom but using every tool at their disposal, whether through escape, sabotage, or rebellion.

Though Hercules's exact fate after his escape remains unknown, it is likely that he lived the rest of his life as a free man, at least for some time. It is possible that he remained in Philadelphia or moved to another northern city where the risk of recapture was lower. Despite the legal and physical dangers of being a fugitive, Hercules's flight from Mount Vernon was an act of unparalleled bravery.

In the years that followed, Washington became increasingly concerned about the fate of his enslaved people and made efforts to ensure that none would escape. Washington's will stipulated that his enslaved people would be freed after Martha Washington's death, but by the time of his passing in 1799, Hercules was already free.

Although the Washingtons did eventually free their slaves upon Martha's death in 1802, Hercules's escape predates this event, and it remains one of the earliest acts of defiance against the first family of the United States. His decision to flee was not merely an attempt to escape physical bondage but a rejection of the hypocrisy that allowed freedom to flourish for some while it was denied to others.

Hercules's story is one of quiet heroism—of a man who, though born into bondage, used his wit, his skill, and his knowledge of the world to claim his freedom. His escape is a testament to the resilience of enslaved people who found ways to resist their captivity in both large and small acts. While Hercules may have been just a chef to George Washington, he was, in fact, a man who defied the expectations of his time, claiming his autonomy and his dignity in a world that sought to strip him of both.

In the context of American history, Hercules's escape represents the many untold stories of enslaved individuals who fought back against a system that denied them basic human rights. Hercules's flight to freedom, like that of so many others, stands as a powerful reminder that even in the face of overwhelming oppression, the will to be free cannot be extinguished.

Gabriel Prosser's Rebellion of 1800

Gabriel's Rebellion, also known as Gabriel Prosser's Rebellion, was a slave uprising that took place in Virginia in the summer of 1800. Despite its failure, the plot, led by an enslaved Black man named Gabriel Prosser, is one of the most important acts of resistance in the history of slavery in the United States. Gabriel's ambition and courage to challenge the system of slavery would make him a symbol of resistance for generations to come, even though the rebellion never fully materialized.

The rebellion has remained significant in American history because it was one of the first major conspiracies among enslaved people that brought the abolitionist cause to the forefront. It exemplified the deep dissatisfaction and unyielding resistance that enslaved people felt toward the conditions of their bondage, and it helped spark a growing fear among white slaveholders in the South, leading to tighter controls on enslaved populations.

This chapter explores the life of Gabriel Prosser, the development of his rebellion, the events surrounding it, and its long-lasting impact on the resistance to slavery.

Gabriel Prosser was born into slavery around 1776 in Henrico County, Virginia. He was the son of an enslaved woman named Giles, and it is likely that he was born to a relatively well-to-do plantation owner. Gabriel was enslaved by

61

Thomas Prosser, a wealthy tobacco farmer, but Gabriel's master allowed him some privileges, including a degree of literacy. Literacy, even in its most basic form, was rare among enslaved persons, but Gabriel learned to read and write and became aware of the world beyond his master's plantation.

Gabriel grew up at a time when the idea of liberty and equality was gaining ground in America. The American Revolution (1775–1783) had introduced ideals of freedom, democracy, and self-determination, and Gabriel, like many other enslaved people, likely felt the bitter irony of these ideals in relation to his own captivity. By the time Gabriel reached adulthood, the United States was a young nation struggling with the contradiction between the pursuit of liberty and the continued practice of slavery. These contradictions would form the intellectual backdrop for Gabriel's rebellion.

Virginia, at the time, had one of the largest enslaved populations in the United States. The state was both the heart of Southern agriculture and a major site of the domestic slave trade. Although enslaved people in Virginia were a significant part of the workforce, they were also keenly aware of their condition and the brutality of their servitude. Gabriel, like other enslaved individuals, was aware of the growing abolitionist movement in the North and the calls for emancipation. He was inspired not just by the ideals of the Revolution, but by the successes of other slave revolts, such as the Haitian Revolution (1791–1804), where enslaved people successfully overthrew their colonial rulers and established an independent republic.

However, Gabriel's rebellion did not spring from abstract political ideals alone. It was deeply personal. The constant brutality of slavery— marked by physical abuse, forced labor, and the separation of families— that he endured fueled Gabriel's determination to fight for his freedom and that of others. With this desire for freedom, Gabriel began to plan a rebellion that would challenge the entire institution of slavery.

In 1800, Gabriel began to organize a rebellion with the aim of freeing the enslaved population in Virginia and, more specifically, in the Richmond area. His plan was simple but audacious: Gabriel and his followers would seize control of the city of Richmond, capture the governor, James Monroe, and force the Virginia legislature to free all enslaved people in the state. He intended to unite enslaved people from the surrounding plantations, particularly those in Henrico County, and involve them in the insurrection.

Gabriel's plan relied on the support of both enslaved and free African people, who were in various stages of resistance against slavery. To coordinate the uprising, Gabriel and his followers communicated through a network of trusted individuals. They used secret meetings and messages, including coded letters and signs, to keep the rebellion a secret.

Gabriel believed that by taking Richmond, he could send a clear message to the state and the country that enslaved people would no longer tolerate the system of oppression that kept them in bondage. He also believed that by capturing prominent white leaders, including the governor, the rebellion would gain the attention and support of the broader population. Gabriel even planned to declare a new government, which would abolish slavery and provide freedom to all enslaved people. He envisioned a new Virginia, where Black people would be treated as equals and where freedom was not confined to a select few.

However, Gabriel's plans began to unravel when, just days before the rebellion was to take place, the plot was exposed. It is unclear exactly who betrayed the rebellion, but the conspiracy was uncovered when one of the conspirators— likely out of fear or personal disagreement— revealed the plan to a white man. The news quickly spread, and local authorities moved to thwart the rebellion.

On August 30, 1800, the authorities in Richmond learned of the plot and took immediate action. Local militia and government officials arrested and interrogated dozens of people involved in the conspiracy. Gabriel was forced to go into hiding, but he was captured shortly afterward, along with several of his co-conspirators. The crackdown was swift and severe. Dozens of enslaved people were arrested and tried for their involvement in the conspiracy.

Gabriel, along with about 26 other men, was tried and convicted of treason. Gabriel was executed by hanging on October 7, 1800. His

64

death marked the end of the rebellion, but it also intensified the fear of slave uprisings among white Virginians and Southern slaveholders. In the aftermath, the state of Virginia enacted even harsher slave laws, restricting the movements and rights of enslaved people and making it more difficult for them to organize or communicate.

In addition to the immediate executions, the state government also imposed restrictions on free Black people, making it harder for them to live in the state and increasing surveillance of enslaved people. These laws, which were meant to prevent future uprisings, made it more difficult for enslaved individuals to gain the resources or support necessary to mount a rebellion.

Although Gabriel's Rebellion was ultimately unsuccessful, it left a profound legacy. Gabriel Prosser's bravery, vision, and determination were a rallying cry for future generations of Black Americans who fought against slavery. The rebellion highlighted the growing discontent among enslaved people and the increasing realization that slavery was not an immutable institution but one that could be challenged and overthrown.

Gabriel's Rebellion also exposed the vulnerabilities in the system of slavery. The fact that an enslaved man could organize a rebellion and almost succeed in overthrowing the government of Virginia spoke to the deep fears of slaveholders about the loyalty of their enslaved populations. The rebellion was one of many factors that influenced the increasing militarization of the South, as states began to implement even more draconian laws to suppress slave revolts.

Gabriel's legacy was carried forward by other prominent figures in the abolitionist movement, including Frederick Douglass, who would later cite the rebellion as a testament to the spirit of resistance that ran through the veins of enslaved Africans. His story was also an inspiration to many enslaved people who, like Gabriel, dreamed of freedom and equality.

Gabriel Prosser's vision of freedom—while not realized in his time—served as a reminder to future generations that the struggle against slavery would continue, no matter how many rebellions were crushed. His story is part of the broader narrative of Black resistance and the unyielding desire for freedom that culminated in the eventual abolition of slavery in the United States.

Gabriel Prosser may not have lived to see the freedom he fought for, but his rebellion remains an indelible part of American history. His courage in the face of nearly impossible odds is a powerful symbol of the will to resist oppression. Gabriel's Rebellion, though thwarted, signaled that the struggle for freedom would continue— and that the fight against slavery was far from over. His actions remind us that resistance takes many forms, from overt rebellion to quiet acts of defiance, and that the hope for freedom can never be fully extinguished.

Charles Deslondes and the German Coast, Louisiana Slave Revolt of 1811

Charles Deslondes, a name often overshadowed by other figures in the history of slave resistance, led one of the largest and most significant uprisings in U.S. history—the 1811 German Coast Uprising. This revolt marked a turning point in the history of slave resistance in Louisiana and remains a powerful symbol of the unyielding fight for freedom against an oppressive system. Deslondes' leadership, his vision for a united uprising, and the fierce, brutal crackdown that followed his revolt reflect the harsh realities and deep tensions of the time.

This chapter explores the life of Charles Deslondes, the events surrounding the 1811 German Coast Uprising, and the enduring legacy of his resistance against the institution of slavery.

Charles Deslondes was born in the late 18th century, likely around 1790, in the French colony of Saint-Domingue (modern-day Haiti), which was then a center of the brutal sugar trade and the epicenter of the Haitian Revolution (1791–1804). Like many individuals of African descent in the Caribbean, Deslondes came from a history of resistance. The Haitian Revolution, which resulted in the establishment of the first independent Black republic, must have had a significant influence on his worldview.

Deslondes was of mixed race, possibly the son of a French planter and an enslaved woman.

67

He was brought to Louisiana—then a French colony and later a part of the United States after the Louisiana Purchase in 1803—at a young age. He was enslaved on a large plantation along the German Coast of the Mississippi River, in what is now St. John the Baptist Parish, Louisiana. The German Coast was a prosperous agricultural region, with vast plantations growing sugarcane, rice, and indigo, all relying on the brutal labor of enslaved Africans and African Americans.

Deslondes grew up under the harsh conditions typical of a large slaveholding plantation, but he was known to be an educated and capable man. He spoke both French and Spanish and had experience working as a driver (a term used for a foreman or overseer on plantations). These skills made him stand out, and it is likely that they gave him the opportunity to develop a vision for resistance.

Like many other enslaved people, Deslondes sought more than just personal freedom. He recognized the deep injustices and violence inherent in the system of slavery, and as he matured, he began to contemplate the possibility of resistance—not just as an isolated act, but as a collective uprising that could lead to a mass liberation of enslaved people.

In the years leading up to the 1811 uprising, tensions among Louisiana's enslaved population were rising. Many of the enslaved people on the German Coast had newly arrived from Haiti, many of whom had experienced the Haitian Revolution firsthand or were influenced by its ideals of liberty and equality. These new

68

arrivals were often more radical in their aspirations, as they had witnessed the success of a large-scale slave revolt and the creation of a free Black republic.

In 1811, the time seemed ripe for such a revolt. The region had a large, enslaved population, many of whom were dissatisfied with their brutal treatment. The instability in the region, as well as a growing racial consciousness among enslaved people, added to the ferment. Charles Deslondes, along with other enslaved leaders, began to organize a rebellion with the aim of freeing enslaved people, marching to New Orleans, and overthrowing the system of slavery in the region.

On January 8, 1811, Deslondes and an estimated 200–500 enslaved people rose up in the German Coast. Armed with machetes, axes, and other improvised weapons, they began marching south toward New Orleans. They initially gathered support from other enslaved people on neighboring plantations, swelling their ranks and growing more confident as they marched. The rebellion was fueled not just by a desire for freedom but also by a broader vision of creating a free Black republic in the region, similar to what had been achieved in Haiti.

Deslondes and his followers set fire to plantation homes, killed several white overseers, and liberated a number of enslaved individuals along the way. As the rebellion gained momentum, the insurgents clashed with local militia and white settlers who attempted to resist their advance. Deslondes' leadership and his

69

ability to inspire and organize the enslaved were critical factors in the revolt's early success.

However, despite their initial successes, the rebellion faced overwhelming opposition. The white plantation owners and militia from New Orleans quickly organized a counteroffensive. On January 10, 1811, the Louisiana militia, bolstered by local planters and armed with cannons, confronted the rebels. The rebellion was decisively crushed in the Battle of the Baton Rouge Road, where many of Deslondes' followers were killed or captured.

After the defeat of the rebels, Charles Deslondes managed to escape for a short period but was eventually captured. His capture, along with the capture of several of his fellow leaders, marked the end of the German Coast Uprising. Deslondes was brought to New Orleans, where he was put on trial.

During his trial, Deslondes did not apologize for his actions; instead, he defended his efforts as a necessary fight for freedom. He believed that the violence he had committed was justified by the larger goal of liberation and that enslaved people had the right to revolt against their oppressors. Despite his defense, he was sentenced to death. On January 26, 1811, Charles Deslondes was executed by hanging—a brutal end to his short-lived but courageous revolt.

The German Coast Uprising was one of the largest slave revolts in U.S. history, yet it ended in failure and retribution. In the aftermath, the plantation economy of Louisiana tightened its grip on the enslaved population. The revolt prompted a harsh crackdown on enslaved people across the region, with many enslaved individuals being punished and killed. Several leaders of the uprising were executed or subjected to gruesome public executions, meant to serve as a warning to anyone else who might consider rebellion.

The uprising also led to tighter restrictions on enslaved people's movements, speech, and gatherings. However, while the immediate result of the uprising was increased repression, the event left an indelible mark on the history of slave resistance.

Though Charles Deslondes' revolt was ultimately unsuccessful, his bravery and the determination of those who followed him made it a significant moment in the history of resistance to slavery. His actions were a powerful reminder to the slaveholding South that enslaved people were not passive victims, but active agents capable of challenging the very foundation of the institution.

Deslondes' revolt was one of many uprisings and rebellions that contributed to the broader abolitionist movement in the United States. His name has been increasingly recognized by historians and activists as an emblem of the struggle for freedom, showing that enslaved people were not simply victims, but agents of their own liberation.

Charles Deslondes may not have achieved his goal of liberating the enslaved people of the

German Coast, but his rebellion remains a testament to the deep and enduring desire for freedom. His actions, although tragic and ultimately unsuccessful, stand as a proud chapter in the history of resistance to slavery.

Deslondes' courage and vision for a free Black republic reflect the broader legacy of uprisings that spread across the Americas during the era of slavery. While his rebellion was violently suppressed, the memory of his leadership has continued to inspire generations of people struggling for freedom, justice, and equality.

Charles Deslondes, like other freedom fighters of his time, understood that true liberation required not just the dismantling of an oppressive system, but also the creation of something new—something more just, more humane, and more equal. His rebellion, though crushed by violence, remains a powerful symbol of the ongoing struggle for human dignity and the fight for liberation against systemic oppression.

Slaves in the Natchez Region Rebel During the War of 1812

The War of 1812, fought between the United States and Great Britain, had far-reaching effects beyond the conventional battlefields of North America. While the United States was engaged in military conflicts with British forces, the war also provided an opportunity for various Native American groups, including the Creeks and Choctaws, to act against the encroachment of American settlers. At the same time, enslaved people throughout the American South were observing the conflict with keen interest, seeing in the chaos a potential moment to break free from the system of slavery that had long bound them. In the Natchez region of Mississippi, this moment would lead to a conspiracy that would attempt to capitalize on the turmoil of war—an alliance between enslaved people, Creek warriors, and the French to strike against the American settler state.

By 1814, the Natchez region in southwestern Mississippi was deeply embedded in the plantation economy, with large numbers of enslaved African Americans laboring on the cotton and tobacco fields of wealthy landowners. The area had long been a hub for trade, agriculture, and political maneuvering, with the Mississippi River serving as a vital route for transporting goods to and from New Orleans. With slavery entrenched as the backbone of this economy, the enslaved population in the region was both large and highly controlled, their lives marked by forced labor, brutal overseers, and systemic violence.

In the broader context of the War of 1812, tensions were high across the American South. The British, seeking to undermine American expansion, allied with various Native American groups in a series of raids and attacks on frontier settlements. Among these groups, the Creek Nation, which had long been in conflict with settlers encroaching on their land, played a significant role. Many Creek warriors, under the leadership of figures like Red Stick leader William Weatherford, had been engaged in violent resistance against American forces, known as the Creek War (1813-1814), which was part of the larger conflict between the United States and Britain.

Meanwhile, the French influence in Louisiana remained strong, despite the territory being formally part of the United States. The French had longstanding ties to many Indigenous groups, and there was a sense among enslaved people that the French might be willing to support uprisings against the U.S. government in exchange for reasserting their influence over the region. The enslaved Africans in the Natchez area, aware of these geopolitical tensions, began to dream of a moment when they might escape their servitude and find a path to freedom, either through violent revolt or by allying with these external powers.

In the spring of 1814, a small but significant conspiracy began to form among the enslaved population in the Natchez region. This

74

plot was not simply the work of a few isolated individuals; it represented a larger, coordinated effort to unite enslaved people, Native American groups, and even French expatriates to overthrow the American slave-holding class and destabilize the fledgling nation. The conspirators hoped to capitalize on the distractions of the War of 1812 and the military conflict between the United States and Britain to strike at their enslavers and seize their freedom.

The plot centered on several key ideas: first, that a large-scale rebellion could be coordinated among the enslaved people in the region; second, that this rebellion would align with Native American warriors, particularly those of the Creek Nation, who were engaged in their own war with the United States; and third, that the French, who had a history of supporting uprisings in the region, might assist in the attack or offer sanctuary to the rebels. The ultimate goal was not only to overthrow the enslavers in the Natchez region but to disrupt the American economy and potentially create a larger insurrection that could spread across the South.

The leaders of the conspiracy among the enslaved people were drawn from various backgrounds—some were African-born, while others were born in the United States or had been born into slavery in the region. The plan was to use the chaos of war to their advantage, attacking key plantations and seizing arms, food, and supplies. They believed that by striking swiftly, they could weaken the control of plantation owners and potentially join forces with Creek warriors who were already in conflict with

75

American forces. The hope was that the combination of Indigenous fighters, enslaved rebels, and French support would lead to a rebellion that could challenge the dominance of U.S. settlers in the region.

The plan included the seizure of critical supply lines, the capture of the town of Natchez itself, and a coordinated attack on local plantations. The conspirators believed that if they could win control of the town, they could use it as a base for further action and as a symbol of resistance to U.S. expansion.

As the plot began to take shape, it did not go undetected for long. The intricate networks of overseers, slave patrols, and informants that plantation owners had put in place to monitor the enslaved population were effective in uncovering conspiracies, even those that seemed well-hidden. The details of how the conspiracy was exposed remain unclear, but it is likely that an informant within the enslaved population or a mistake made by one of the plotters led to the discovery. In any case, by mid-1814, the authorities were aware of the threat.

In response, local authorities, including plantation owners and the military, swiftly acted to put down the conspiracy. They arrested several suspected conspirators and began interrogating enslaved people who were believed to have been involved. The French presence in Louisiana had long been a source of tension for the U.S. government, and any hint of French support for rebellion or unrest in the region was treated with extreme suspicion. As a result, a coordinated crackdown was launched to prevent further uprisings and isolate the leaders of the conspiracy.

The response to the conspiracy was swift and brutal. Authorities immediately tightened security in the Natchez region, increasing patrols and surveillance of the enslaved population. Plantation owners and overseers were put on high alert, and the potential for wider uprisings was taken very seriously.

The enslaved people suspected of being involved in the conspiracy were arrested, and many were subjected to violent interrogations. Some were executed, either hanged or shot, as a means of deterring others from following in their footsteps. Others were sent to prison or forced into hard labor, where they were kept under stricter supervision. Entire families of those accused of being involved were often punished, even if they had not participated directly in the conspiracy.

The authorities also took steps to dismantle the broader network that had supported the rebellion. They cracked down on communication among enslaved people, increasing punishment for any forms of resistance, including secret meetings or whispered conversations. Many of the enslaved population were relocated to other plantations or sent further south, away from areas where they might have contact with sympathetic Native groups or the French.

While the plot in the Natchez region was foiled, it was far from an isolated incident.

Throughout the War of 1812, there were a number of similar conspiracies and uprisings among enslaved people, many of whom saw the chaos of war as an opportunity for rebellion. The desire for freedom, stoked by promises of assistance from foreign powers or Indigenous allies, was a potent force. In many cases, enslaved people in the South hoped to join forces with Native American groups who were engaged in their own wars against the United States, seeing their struggles as interconnected.

The failure of the Natchez rebellion, along with other failed conspiracies in the region, did not silence the desire for freedom. Instead, it sowed deeper resentment and fueled a growing sense of solidarity among enslaved people across the South. Over the next several decades, slave resistance would continue to manifest in various forms, from small acts of sabotage to larger, more organized uprisings like the Denmark Vesey plot in 1822 and Nat Turner's Rebellion in 1831.

For the enslaved people of the Natchez region in 1814, the conspiracy was ultimately crushed, but their willingness to resist oppression at all costs remained a powerful symbol of defiance against the system of slavery.

The 1814 conspiracy in the Natchez region stands as one of the many expressions of resistance by enslaved people in the American South. Though the plot was suppressed before it could achieve its goals, it highlighted the lengths to which enslaved people were willing to go to secure their freedom, even in the midst of a global conflict like the War of 1812. By attempting to ally

78

with the Creek Nation and the French, the enslaved rebels in Natchez were not only seeking to escape their own oppression but also hoped to undermine the broader structure of colonial domination that kept them in bondage. Their actions, while ultimately unsuccessful, are a testament to the unyielding desire for freedom that would continue to drive resistance movements in the years to come.

Denmark Vesey and the Charleston Slave Conspiracy of 1822

Denmark Vesey is one of the most significant figures in the history of slave resistance in the United States, his name synonymous with defiance, hope, and a daring vision of freedom. The conspiracy he led in 1822—one of the largest slave revolts planned in American history—highlighted the complexity and urgency of the enslaved people's desire for liberation and the fierce lengths to which they would go to reclaim their autonomy. This chapter delves into the life, actions, and legacy of Denmark Vesey, examining the context of his revolt, the forces that shaped his leadership, and the impact his conspiracy had on the history of slavery in America.

Denmark Vesey was born circa 1767 in the Danish West Indies, specifically on the island of St. Thomas. His birth name was Telemaque, a reflection of his Afro-Caribbean heritage. He was enslaved at a young age and brought to Charleston, South Carolina, where he was sold to a man named Captain Joseph Vesey. It was here that he took on the name Denmark Vesey.

Vesey's early life was marked by hardship and subjugation, but his intellectual and personal strength began to emerge. As a young man, he was able to save enough money through his work as a carpenter to purchase his freedom in 1799, after being enslaved for more than 30 years. Vesey's emancipation was a significant

80

achievement, but it was also a source of frustration for him. He lived in a society where racial oppression was deeply entrenched, and even as a free Black man, he faced constant discrimination. The system of slavery was an ever-present force in his life, shaping his worldview and fueling his desire to see it destroyed.

As a free man, Vesey was able to establish himself as a carpenter, which made him reasonably prosperous for a Black man in Charleston. He also became active in the city's African Methodist Episcopal (AME) Church, where he rose to a position of prominence as a lay preacher. The AME Church, which was founded by free and enslaved Black people, became a space for Vesey to articulate his views on freedom, justice, and religion. His sermons, which espoused Christian values of equality, justice, and liberation, resonated deeply with other enslaved and free Black people in Charleston.

Through his religious and social networks, Vesey became acquainted with many other free and enslaved Black individuals who shared his desire for freedom. It was within these circles that he began to organize for what would become the infamous Denmark Vesey Slave Conspiracy of 1822.

The year 1822 was a period of increasing racial tension in Charleston. The city was home to a large, enslaved population, and many of them, like Vesey, were deeply dissatisfied with their lives. The domestic and international climate also played a role in fueling discontent.

The Haitian Revolution (1791–1804), which had successfully overthrown French colonial rule in the Caribbean and established the first independent Black republic, served as a powerful inspiration to enslaved Black people throughout the Americas. Vesey, who had likely heard of the Haitian Revolution, was motivated by the example of Haitian freedom fighters and saw a similar possibility for revolt in Charleston.

Vesey's plan was nothing short of audacious. He envisioned a large-scale uprising in which enslaved people would rise up, seize arms, and overthrow their masters. His goal was to take control of Charleston, liberate the enslaved population, and establish a free Black republic. The plot was to involve a number of enslaved people from various walks of life: house slaves, field workers, craftsmen, and even free Black men who would act as strategists and organizers.

Vesey's rebellion was carefully planned, with a timeline set for the uprising to take place on the Fourth of July 1822, a day symbolizing freedom and independence in the United States. He aimed to strike when the city would be least prepared for such an insurrection, believing that the distraction of the holiday celebrations would create an opportunity for a swift and effective takeover.

The conspiracy was not limited to Charleston itself; Vesey had made contacts with other enslaved individuals in surrounding areas, including plantations in nearby districts. His plan was to arm himself and his followers with weapons from local arsenals, then burn the city, kill key white figures, and seize control of strategic locations.

Despite Vesey's meticulous planning and widespread support, the conspiracy was doomed to failure, not because of the lack of bravery or resolve, but because of betrayal. A fellow conspirator, possibly out of fear or self-interest, revealed the plot to the authorities.

The betrayal of the conspiracy led to a swift and brutal response from Charleston's authorities. Vesey and many of his co-conspirators were arrested, and the city was thrown into a state of panic. The authorities, fearing the rebellion would spark a much larger revolt across the South, acted quickly to crush any remaining signs of insurrection.

Vesey's trial became a spectacle of fear and oppression. He was accused of masterminding the revolt, and his actions were framed as an attack on the very fabric of Southern society. In his trial, Vesey remained resolute and unwavering in his beliefs. He admitted to organizing the plot, though he denied that he intended to use violence against the enslaved people. His defense, which portrayed the conspiracy as a rightful act of rebellion, did little to sway the court.

In the end, Denmark Vesey and 34 other conspirators were found guilty of treason, conspiracy, and incitement to rebellion. Vesey himself was sentenced to death. He was hanged on July 2, 1822, along with many of his co-

conspirators, marking the end of his bold attempt to bring freedom to Charleston's enslaved population.

Vesey's execution sent shockwaves through Charleston and the broader slaveholding South. The city enacted even stricter laws to prevent further revolts. Enslaved people faced increased surveillance and were subjected to harsher punishments for even the smallest infraction. Black churches, especially the African Methodist Episcopal Church, were scrutinized and heavily restricted, as they had served as a central organizing hub for the conspiracy.

Despite his tragic end, Denmark Vesey's actions reverberated far beyond his death. His revolt became a symbol of Black resistance and a reminder of the latent power of enslaved people. Although the immediate response to the conspiracy was one of heightened repression, Vesey's ideas did not die with him. His vision of a liberated Black community continued to inspire future generations of abolitionists and freedom fighters, including figures like Nat Turner and Frederick Douglass, who would also rise against the institution of slavery.

Vesey's legacy is complex. While he failed in his immediate objective, his attempt to bring freedom to enslaved people in Charleston was an important chapter in the long history of resistance to slavery. His courage, vision, and determination to fight for liberty made him a lasting symbol of resistance and hope for generations to come.

Denmark Vesey's life and the revolt he led challenge the simplistic narrative of passivity often associated with enslaved people. He demonstrated that enslaved individuals, even under the harshest conditions, could rise up against their oppressors with courage, intelligence, and determination. His rebellion was a reflection of the broader resistance movements that grew in the shadow of slavery, laying the groundwork for the abolitionist movements that would later sweep the United States.

Vesey's actions also reminded America of the deep contradictions in its founding ideals. While the nation professed liberty and freedom, those very ideals were denied to millions of enslaved people. The bravery of Denmark Vesey, and his quest for freedom, underscores the ongoing struggle for justice, dignity, and human rights that has defined the history of African Americans.

Denmark Vesey, in his quest for freedom, proved that even in the darkest hours, the spirit of resistance can burn brightly. His legacy lives on as a testament to the unyielding desire for freedom that, despite the many forces designed to crush it, would ultimately lead to the abolition of slavery and the broader struggle for civil rights in America.

Nat Turner's Rebellion of 1831

Nat Turner (1800–1831) is one of the most controversial and enigmatic figures in American history. Born into slavery in Southampton County, Virginia, Turner would go on to lead one of the most significant slave rebellions in the history of the United States. His actions, as well as the subsequent reaction to his rebellion, have had a lasting impact on the nation's conscience, especially in the context of slavery, race relations, and the broader struggle for freedom.

Turner's bravery was not just a matter of physical courage but also intellectual and spiritual resolve. He believed himself to be divinely chosen to lead his people out of bondage, and his rebellion was as much a religious and prophetic act as it was a revolutionary one. His story is one of deep conviction, immense risk, and profound consequences—both for the enslaved and for the institution of slavery itself. This chapter delves into the life of Nat Turner, examining the roots of his courage, the rebellion he led, and his legacy in the ongoing fight for freedom and justice.

Nat Turner was born on October 2, 1800, in Southampton County, Virginia, a region steeped in the horrors of slavery. His mother, Nancy, was enslaved, and his father, who had escaped to freedom when Turner was an infant, was never a part of his life. From an early age, Turner demonstrated unusual intelligence and sensitivity. As a child, he was deeply observant and curious about the world around him. His

86

intelligence caught the attention of his owners, who allowed him to receive a rudimentary education, a privilege that was rare for enslaved people at the time.

Turner's early experiences of witnessing the brutalities of slavery shaped his worldview. He grew up amid constant violence, watching his fellow slaves endure physical punishment, forced labor, and psychological degradation. But it was not just the cruelty of slavery that stirred Turner; it was also the spiritual awakening he experienced as a young man. Turner came to believe that he was chosen by God to lead his people to freedom.

From his teenage years, Turner began to have intense, vivid visions that he interpreted as divine revelations. He believed that God had given him a mission to overthrow the institution of slavery. According to Turner, these visions led him to believe that he was anointed to lead a rebellion that would bring about divine justice for the suffering of Black people.

By 1831, after years of religious contemplation and preparing for his mission, Turner felt the time had come to act. His rebellion would come to be known as Nat Turner's Rebellion, but its planning and execution were not as spontaneous as often portrayed. Turner had been organizing a group of enslaved and free Black men who shared his vision for liberation. They secretly discussed plans, rehearsed their attacks, and waited for a sign from God to take action.

On August 21, 1831, Turner and a small group of followers launched their rebellion in the dead of night. They began at Turner's home in Southampton County, where they first killed his master, Joseph Travis, and his family. From there, the rebellion spread to other neighboring plantations. Over the next 48 hours, Turner and his band of rebels killed around 55 to 65 white people, including men, women, and children. The attackers used axes, guns, and knives to carry out their mission, which was driven by a combination of religious fervor and a desire to punish those responsible for the enslavement of Black people.

Turner's leadership and the speed of the rebellion initially stunned the local white population. The rebels moved from one plantation to the next, freeing enslaved people and rallying more followers. However, the rebellion was not well coordinated beyond the initial stages, and Turner's forces were small and outnumbered. White militia forces, along with local militias, quickly mobilized to suppress the uprising.

What sets Nat Turner apart from many other figures in history is not just his action but his deep belief in the righteousness of his cause. His bravery was not simply about armed confrontation; it was rooted in his spiritual conviction and his understanding of his role in the fight for liberation.

Turner's courage was most evident in his unwavering commitment to his cause. He did not back down in the face of overwhelming opposition. Despite being pursued by armed militias, he continued to fight, believing that his actions were divinely inspired and that his cause was just. Turner was aware of the risks involved, including the brutal reprisals that would surely follow any attempt at rebellion. But his resolve was absolute.

After the initial violence, the rebellion's momentum began to wane. By August 23, 1831, Turner's group was defeated, and many of his followers were captured or killed. Turner himself went into hiding, but he was eventually discovered on October 30, 1831, after nearly two months on the run. When he was captured, Turner remained calm and resolute. He did not apologize or renounce his actions, and he remained steadfast in his belief that the rebellion had been divinely ordained.

After his capture, Turner was put on trial for his role in the rebellion. He was convicted of insurrection and murder and sentenced to death. On November 11, 1831, Nat Turner was executed by hanging. We hold him today as a hero and martyr.

Despite his death, the rebellion did not go unnoticed. The aftermath of the rebellion sent shockwaves through the South, sparking a wave of repression. In the wake of the rebellion, Southern states passed even harsher laws aimed at controlling enslaved and free Black populations. These laws restricted Black people's rights to assembly, education, and movement. White militias were formed, and retaliatory violence against Black communities escalated, leading to the deaths of hundreds of innocent

Black people who were either directly involved in the rebellion or simply suspected of being sympathetic to it.

However, the fear and panic that the rebellion generated among Southern whites also made it clear that the system of slavery was not invulnerable. Turner's bravery and his willingness to fight back against the brutal institution of slavery inspired others, both during his time and in the years that followed. His rebellion, while ultimately unsuccessful, became a symbol of resistance and a spark for future abolitionist efforts.

Nat Turner's rebellion had profound consequences. While it failed to bring about immediate change, it laid bare the extreme lengths to which enslaved people were willing to go to secure their freedom. It also highlighted the deep fears of white slaveowners and the fragility of the institution of slavery.

Turner's bravery left an indelible mark on the history of American resistance to slavery. In the years following his death, his name became synonymous with slave resistance. Abolitionists, including Frederick Douglass, praised Turner's courage, while pro-slavery advocates viewed him as a dangerous symbol of Black insurrection.

Over time, Turner became a complex figure in American history. For many Black people, he was seen as a hero who had boldly stood up against the system of slavery, risking everything in the pursuit of justice. For white Americans, particularly in the South, he was a symbol of fear and chaos, a reminder of the violence and uprising that lay beneath the surface of the institution of slavery.

In the 20th and 21st centuries, Nat Turner's legacy has been revisited by historians and activists who have sought to reclaim his story from the shadows. In literature, art, and scholarship, Turner is increasingly seen as a figure who challenged not only the physical constraints of slavery but also the spiritual and moral justifications used to perpetuate it.

His actions have been reinterpreted in the context of the larger struggle for Black liberation, and his story is now viewed as part of the broader narrative of resistance to oppression. In this light, Nat Turner's bravery is not just a historical anecdote, but an enduring symbol of the courage required to fight for justice, no matter the cost.

Nat Turner's rebellion is one of the most powerful expressions of resistance in American history. His courage, driven by an unwavering belief in the righteousness of his cause, continues to inspire generations of people fighting for justice and freedom. Although his rebellion was short-lived, the example of his bravery remains a testament to the indomitable spirit of those who fought against the brutal system of slavery.

Turner's story is not one of blind violence but of calculated, spiritual, and prophetic resistance. He understood the enormity of the risk he was taking, yet his commitment to freedom—and his refusal to accept a life of bondage—reveals the true depth of his courage.

As such, Nat Turner remains an enduring symbol of the fight for justice and the unwavering spirit of resistance in the face of oppression.

The Killing of Slave Traders Jesse and John Kirby 1834

Jesse Kirby and John Kirby were two white men from the U.S. state of Georgia who were killed by enslaved persons they were trafficking from Maryland to Georgia. The Killing of the Kirby brothers is an example of captives enslaved of the interstate slave trade conspiring "to kill their enslavers and avoid being subjugated to bondage.

The Kirbys had been to the slave markets of both Baltimore and Chestertown and were traveling with a group of at least nine enslaved Africans through Virginia by coffle. To coffle was to chain enslaved human beings together by their hands and feet, and force them to walk treacherous hours for miles, often several states at a time. The Kirbys were killed at an overnight campsite near Prince Edward County, Virginia, by their captives. A Virginia newspaper highlighting the killings headlined "Horrid Outrage" and reported, "Their throats were cut, and the head of one cleft open with an ax." An enslaved woman named Rachel later described how "their heads were broken, faces bloody, and brains knocked out."

The Governor of Virginia offered a $200 (equivalent to $6,800 in 2025) reward for the men believed responsible: George and Littleton. George had reportedly been in Philadelphia, Pennsylvania for several years and deemed a runaway. Littleton was described as a younger and more frail "dark mulatto" Also with group was Moses, Horace, George Jr., Julia Ann

93

and her two-year-old child, and "Matilda, a bright mulatto girl, about 10 years old." They not only killed them but made sure to take the Kirbys' pistol, cash, and clothing for provisional needs. The *Farmville Journal*, by way of the *North Carolina Star*, in May of 1834, stated that seven of the eight enslaved were recaptured together, in possession of $582 that had been carried by the Kirbys. Certainly, a hefty sum to travel with in the year 1834. The eighth member of the group had recaptured separately. Per the *Farmville Journal*, "Four of them have confessed their guilt." According to newspaper, the killings were said to have occurred an hour before dawn.

The records of the subsequent court cases reported that the murders happened in the evening, after dinner; the bodies were discovered when "the scream of a young slave boy jolted everyone awake." Slaves working "collectively" to do violence to "cruel owners" was a comparative "rarity" in the history of antebellum violence by the enslaved in Virginia, but "Having left Maryland and their homes behind, [George, Little and their allies] likely believed that violence afforded them the last possible opportunity to escape whatever fate awaited them in Georgia. Georgia offered fewer opportunities for escape than Maryland. The movement south threw the slaves lives into flux." From statehood until 1856, it was illegal to import slaves into Georgia "except for personal use.

Slave Revolt in the Cherokee Nation 1842

In the early 19th century, the Cherokee Nation in Indian Territory (modern-day Oklahoma) was undergoing profound social and political transformation. The forced relocation known as the *Trail of Tears* had displaced the Cherokee people from their ancestral lands in the Southeastern United States to Indian Territory. Among the consequences of this relocation was the development of a system of plantation agriculture, where enslaved African Americans were brought to work on the farms and plantations of wealthy Cherokee families. One of the most significant events that would challenge the emerging power structure of the Cherokee Nation was the 1842 slave revolt at the Joseph Vann plantation.

By the time of the 1842 revolt, the Cherokee Nation had been forcibly relocated from their homeland in Georgia, Tennessee, North Carolina, and Alabama. The *Trail of Tears*, which took place between 1838 and 1839, resulted in the death of thousands of Cherokees during their forced migration to Indian Territory. Once settled in their new land, the Cherokee Nation struggled to rebuild their lives, adopting elements of Western-style agriculture, governance, and economy. This process was heavily influenced by the adoption of slave labor, a practice that had already existed in the South for generations.

While not all Cherokee people practiced slavery, a significant number of wealthy Cherokee

95

men and women, including the elite class of "civilized" Cherokees, embraced plantation agriculture. Joseph Vann, the primary figure in the 1842 slave revolt, was a prominent member of this elite class. Vann had inherited a large plantation near the confluence of the Illinois and Arkansas rivers in Indian Territory, where he operated a thriving cotton farm with the labor of enslaved African Americans.

Vann's plantation was one of the largest and most prosperous in the region. At its peak, it housed over 100 enslaved people, and his wealth made him a powerful figure in the political and economic life of the Cherokee Nation. Vann's plantation represented the integration of slavery into the fabric of Cherokee society, despite the complexity of this relationship. For many Cherokees, slavery was viewed as a necessary institution to emulate the plantation economy of the American South, and it was a source of considerable tension both within the tribe and in relations with neighboring nations.

However, for the enslaved people who were brought to Indian Territory, life was one of brutal labor, harsh conditions, and limited hope for freedom. Despite this, the enslaved African Americans living on plantations like Vann's were not passive in their suffering. They found ways to resist, and the 1842 slave revolt would be one of the most significant acts of resistance in the history of the Cherokee Nation.

Joseph Vann's plantation was strategically located in Indian Territory, an area that was rich in resources and perfect for the cultivation of cotton, a crop that was central to the plantation economy of the South. The enslaved people who worked on Vann's plantation were subjected to long hours of grueling labor in the fields, with minimal oversight and little regard for their well-being.

Vann, who was known for his wealth and social standing, was also notorious for his brutal treatment of enslaved individuals. Like many slaveholders in the region, Vann was determined to maintain control over his workers and protect his financial interests. His plantation was not just a symbol of prosperity; it was also a site of extreme exploitation.

The enslaved men and women who lived under Vann's authority endured constant surveillance, limited freedom, and the ever-present threat of violence. They were not just property; they were vital to the functioning of the plantation economy. However, they were also human beings capable of resistance, even under the most oppressive conditions.

The slave revolt that occurred at Joseph Vann's plantation in 1842 was not an isolated incident, but part of a larger wave of resistance movements among enslaved people across the South and the Indian Territory. Enslaved African Americans found various ways to rebel—whether through subtle acts of resistance like slowdowns and sabotage or through more direct means, such as uprisings.

In the case of the 1842 revolt, the enslaved people at Vann's plantation decided they could no

97

longer endure the harsh conditions imposed upon them. Accounts of the revolt are sparse and often contradictory, but the basic details suggest that a group of enslaved men and women, tired of their treatment, planned and executed a rebellion against their enslavers. It appears that the revolt was sparked by a combination of factors: the brutal treatment they endured, the increasing number of enslaved individuals on the plantation, and the growing tensions between the enslaved and their masters.

On the night of the revolt, the enslaved people on Vann's plantation rose up. They killed several overseers and freed some of their fellow enslaved people, taking control of the plantation for a brief period. The nature of the revolt was sudden and violent, and it sent shockwaves throughout the Cherokee community.

However, the revolt did not go unnoticed. Vann and his allies, including other wealthy Cherokee slaveholders, quickly mobilized a response. The Cherokee authorities, who were invested in maintaining their power structure and their economic ties to slavery, took swift action. A group of armed Cherokee men, including some of Vann's relatives, were sent to put down the uprising. The rebellion was swiftly crushed, and many of the enslaved individuals who had participated were either killed or captured and returned to servitude.

While the revolt was short-lived, it had lasting effects on the Cherokee Nation. In the immediate aftermath, the rebel slaves were punished, and strict measures were put in place to prevent further uprisings. Slave patrols became more frequent, and overseers were given additional power to maintain control over the enslaved people.

Despite the defeat, the revolt highlighted the deepening divisions within the Cherokee Nation. The existence of slavery in Indian Territory was an issue that continued to divide the Cherokee people. Some Cherokee leaders, including Principal Chief John Ross, were opposed to slavery, but many of the wealthier elites saw it as essential to their economic survival. The revolt at the Joseph Vann plantation further revealed the tensions between these factions, as well as the growing recognition among enslaved people that they could resist their conditions, even in the face of overwhelming odds.

In the broader context of the Indian Territory, the 1842 revolt also became part of the larger resistance movement among enslaved African Americans in the United States. While the rebellion in the Cherokee Nation did not result in the immediate emancipation of enslaved people, it was part of the growing wave of resistance that would eventually culminate in the Civil War and the abolition of slavery.

The 1842 revolt also marked a pivotal moment in the history of the Cherokee Nation's relationship with slavery. Although the practice continued to thrive for several more decades, the revolt served as a reminder of the fragile power structures built on the backs of enslaved laborers and the unyielding desire for freedom among those who were oppressed.

The 1842 slave revolt at Joseph Vann's plantation is a stark reminder of the complexities and contradictions of slavery in the Cherokee Nation. It also highlights the resilience and courage of enslaved African Americans who resisted their enslavement at great personal risk. Although the revolt was crushed, it left an indelible mark on the Cherokee Nation, further complicating the tribe's identity and relationship to slavery as they continued to navigate the pressures of survival and assimilation in a changing world.

In examining the revolt, we are not only reminded of the brutality of the plantation system but also of the agency and resistance that existed even in the most oppressive of circumstances. The story of the 1842 revolt is one of struggle, defiance, and the enduring hope for freedom, themes that continue to resonate in the broader narrative of American history.

The Creole Mutiny of 1841

The history of the transatlantic slave trade is marked by violence, exploitation, and suffering, but it is also defined by the courage of those who sought to resist and break free from the chains of slavery. One of the most remarkable and dramatic episodes in this long struggle for freedom occurred aboard the *Creole*, a U.S.-owned ship, in 1841. The events surrounding the *Creole* mutiny remain one of the most audacious acts of rebellion in the history of enslaved peoples, illustrating both the deep resilience of those who had been bound by slavery and the immense stakes of the international battle over human freedom.

The *Creole* was a slave ship, a vessel traveling from Washington, D.C. to New Orleans. On board was a cargo of 135 enslaved people, bound for sale in the southern United States, which was notorious for its brutal system of chattel slavery. The captain and crew were tasked with transporting these human beings as though they were mere property, to be auctioned off and sold into lives of forced labor on the plantations of the Deep South.

Among the 135 enslaved people on board were a number of individuals who had already suffered the horror of being torn from their homes and families in Africa. They had been forced into servitude, sold to traders, and transported across the Atlantic, where they endured the brutal conditions of the Middle Passage. Now, aboard the *Creole*, many of them found themselves

101

caught in the same cycle of oppression that had characterized their entire lives.

However, among the enslaved people on the *Creole* was a group of men and women who refused to accept their fate without a fight. These individuals would soon make a bold decision that would change their lives—and the course of history—forever.

The *Creole* left Washington, D.C., on October 27, 1841, and began its journey down the Chesapeake Bay, making its way southward. The captain of the ship, Ingraham, was an experienced sailor, and his crew was accustomed to the usual dynamics of slave transport. For most of the enslaved people on board, the journey was yet another harrowing chapter in their lives, one that seemed to offer little hope of escape or reprieve.

But a group of enslaved men, led by a man named Madison Washington, had different plans. Washington was an experienced sailor who had been born into slavery in Virginia. After enduring the brutalities of enslavement, he had escaped, only to be recaptured and sold into a life of even greater hardship. When he was forced aboard the *Creole*, he recognized the opportunity for escape. Washington was a man of immense determination, and when he saw the chance, he seized it.

On the morning of November 7, 1841, as the ship sailed through the waters near the Bahamas, Washington and a group of other enslaved men rose up against their captors. They overpowered the crew, taking control of the ship in an act of defiance and resistance. The mutiny was swift and brutal. Armed with weapons they had seized from the crew, the enslaved people on board took the upper hand, overpowering their captors with surprising force.

The mutiny was a calculated, organized action. Washington's leadership and the unity among the enslaved people on the *Creole* ensured that the revolt was not only successful but also relatively bloodless. While one crew member was killed during the uprising, the mutineers spared most of the others, treating them with surprising restraint. The crew members were soon imprisoned below deck, and the ship's direction was turned toward the British-controlled island of Nassau in the Bahamas.

Once the *Creole* arrived in Nassau, the mutineers sought asylum from the British authorities, who had abolished slavery in their territories in 1834. Nassau, a bustling port city, was a place of refuge for enslaved people who managed to escape the grasp of their captors. Under British law, those who reached British soil were considered free, and the mutineers expected their actions to be validated.

However, the events of the *Creole* mutiny would not unfold as straightforwardly as the insurgents had hoped. Though the mutineers found safety in Nassau, their legal status became a point of contention. The United States, furious over the loss of their property, demanded the return of the *Creole* and the mutineers. The U.S. government insisted that the enslaved people

103

aboard the ship were, in fact, property that had been stolen, and they invoked international treaties with Britain to request their return.

The British authorities in Nassau, however, stood firm. The Bahamas had long been a destination for those escaping slavery, and the British government had no intention of reversing their stance on freedom. Under British law, the mutineers were considered free, and they could not be forcibly returned to slavery. The British insisted that the U.S. had no legal claim over the individuals who had taken part in the mutiny, citing the abolition of slavery in British territories and their commitment to providing refuge to those who escaped bondage.

The legal battle continued for several months, with the U.S. and Britain exchanging diplomatic notes and threats over the situation. Eventually, in the spring of 1842, the British government agreed to release the *Creole* and its remaining crew members, but the enslaved individuals who had participated in the mutiny were allowed to remain free in the Bahamas. The British refusal to return the mutineers was a significant moment in the history of the abolitionist movement, representing a direct challenge to the institution of slavery and the U.S. system of human chattel.

The *Creole* mutiny stands as one of the most successful slave rebellions in history. Unlike other revolts that were crushed by military might, the mutineers of the *Creole* achieved their goal of freedom, escaping from slavery not only physically but also by outmaneuvering their oppressors legally and diplomatically. The rebellion sent shockwaves through the South and the rest of the United States, highlighting the vulnerability of the institution of slavery and the determination of enslaved people to fight for their freedom by any means necessary.

In the broader context of the abolition movement, the *Creole* mutiny served as a powerful reminder that enslaved people were not passive victims, but active agents in their fight for freedom. The bravery of Madison Washington and the other mutineers inspired further resistance, both on the seas and in the streets, contributing to the growing abolitionist sentiment in the United States and abroad.

The events surrounding the *Creole* mutiny would not be the last confrontation between those who sought to preserve slavery and those who fought against it. Just over two decades later, in 1861, the Civil War would break out, and the question of slavery would finally be decided by armed conflict. But in 1841, aboard the *Creole*, enslaved men and women made a powerful statement to the world: the thirst for freedom could not be contained, and the fight for liberty would never cease.

The mutiny marked a moment in history when enslaved people asserted their power in a way that the world could not ignore, showing the world that their resistance, like their spirits, could not be broken.

The Great Slave Stampede of Missouri in 1849

The Great Slave Stampede in Missouri, a daring and lesser-known act of resistance, unfolded in 1841 as one of the most remarkable, yet underreported, instances of mass slave escape in U.S. history. This event involved a large group of enslaved people, primarily from the rural outskirts of Missouri, who made an audacious attempt to escape to freedom in the North. Despite the tremendous risks involved, these brave individuals mounted a mass escape that challenged the brutal system of slavery in the United States, defied the harsh laws of the time, and helped to spark further acts of rebellion and flight.

This chapter delves into the context, the individuals involved, the escape itself, and its aftermath. Through examining the Great Slave Stampede, we gain insight into the ways enslaved people in Missouri—one of the largest slaveholding states on the western frontier—resisted their conditions and sought to secure freedom, even in the face of overwhelming odds.

Missouri, situated at the crossroads of the slaveholding South and the free North, was a pivotal state in the complex dynamics of pre-Civil War America. The state's economy was heavily reliant on agriculture, particularly tobacco, hemp, and cotton, all of which were grown by enslaved labor. By the time of the Great Slave Stampede in 1841, Missouri had one of the largest enslaved populations in the United States.

It was a border state where slavery was legal but where the influence of abolitionist ideas from the North was also palpable.

Missouri was positioned at the boundary between the Missouri Compromise Line—which divided free and slave states—and the free territories to the north. The state's proximity to free states such as Illinois, Iowa, and Ohio made it an important site of conflict between pro-slavery and anti-slavery forces. Slave owners in Missouri, deeply concerned about the potential for escaped slaves to find sanctuary in free states, enacted severe measures to keep their enslaved populations under control, including harsh punishments, strict curfews, and surveillance.

The Mississippi River, which ran along Missouri's eastern edge, was both a physical and symbolic barrier. On the one hand, it served as a route for enslaved people to escape southward into the Deep South, but it was also a critical escape route northward to free states. Enslaved people were acutely aware of the fact that crossing the river could lead them to freedom, but the risk was enormous. Fugitives could be caught at any moment and subjected to severe punishment.

By the 1830s and 1840s, abolitionist sentiment was gaining ground in Missouri, despite the state's entrenched system of slavery. This shifting atmosphere, combined with increasing slave resistance, made Missouri a flashpoint in the struggle for freedom.

In 1841, a mass escape attempt was organized in Missouri—an act that would come to be known as the Great Slave Stampede. A number of enslaved individuals, primarily from St. Charles and St. Louis counties along the Missouri River, formed a large group that planned to escape northward to the free states. It is believed that the conspirators were inspired by previous acts of resistance, such as the underground railroad, and the growing momentum of abolitionist movements, as well as the pressing desire for personal freedom and autonomy.

The plan was audacious: enslaved individuals, many of them women and children, would gather secretly and make a coordinated flight to the north. The escape was organized through secret communication networks, likely utilizing the help of sympathetic free Black people, abolitionists, and perhaps even conductors on the Underground Railroad, who had been known to assist enslaved people escaping the South. The plan involved crossing the Mississippi River at a point where they would be less likely to be detected, and then traveling through the state of Illinois, where they would find safety and freedom.

On the night of the escape, which occurred in the spring of 1841, around 100 enslaved people—mostly from the St. Charles and St. Louis regions—gathered in the darkness of the night to begin their journey. They crossed the river and began their trek northward, some by foot, others on horseback, attempting to avoid patrols and keep out of sight of slave catchers. The escapees' ultimate goal was freedom in the North, either in

Ohio or beyond, where they hoped to find sanctuary in states where slavery had been abolished.

As the group moved northward, they encountered several challenges. One of the most immediate threats was the presence of slave catchers and patrols, who were vigilant for any signs of fleeing slaves. The group faced the daunting task of moving through hostile territory while avoiding detection. They relied on secrecy, speed, and the help of abolitionist allies who had offered refuge along the way.

Unfortunately, the Great Slave Stampede did not succeed in its entirety. While the group had made impressive strides in their journey northward, the authorities in Missouri soon learned of the escape. Slave patrols and bounty hunters were quickly mobilized to track down the runaways, and news of the escape spread quickly among the local white population.

The escapees' flight was short-lived. Within a few days, the Missouri authorities caught wind of the movement and began to close in. In an act of betrayal, it is believed that one of the conspirators—either coerced or motivated by fear—alerted the authorities to the whereabouts of the group. Once this information reached the authorities, they set off in pursuit of the runaways, using dogs and other means to track the group's movement. The escapees were caught and apprehended one by one.

Some were returned to their owners, while others faced violent retaliation. The Missouri authorities did not show mercy: many of the enslaved participants in the Great Slave Stampede were subjected to extreme physical punishment. Some were hanged, others were branded or whipped, while the ringleaders—those thought to have orchestrated the escape—faced the most brutal retribution.

After the stampede failed, the authorities in Missouri enacted even stricter laws aimed at preventing future escape attempts. Slave patrols were increased, and new laws were put in place that prohibited the gathering of enslaved people in large groups. Enslaved people were forbidden from learning to read or write, and severe penalties were imposed on anyone caught aiding a fugitive slave. Those who were suspected of participating in or facilitating an escape could face severe punishments, including death.

However, the Great Slave Stampede also had a longer-lasting impact. Although the immediate outcome was one of failure, the attempt itself was a powerful statement of defiance. It was a reminder to slaveholders in Missouri and throughout the South that the enslaved population would continue to resist their captivity and fight for their freedom, no matter the odds. The event inspired further acts of rebellion and helped to strengthen abolitionist resolve across the North.

The escape attempt also contributed to the growing fear of slave insurrection, which would be one of the factors that contributed to the growing tensions between the North and South leading up to the Civil War. For enslaved people, the Stampede was a powerful reminder that freedom was not simply something to be hoped for, but something worth fighting for at all costs.

The Great Slave Stampede in Missouri, like so many other acts of resistance, has largely been forgotten in mainstream histories of slavery and abolition. Yet, the courage of the individuals involved in this act of defiance speaks to the deep desire for freedom that burned within the hearts of enslaved people. The Stampede was not just an attempt to flee; it was a bold assertion of autonomy and self-determination in the face of one of the most oppressive systems in history.

While the rebellion ultimately failed, the story of the Great Slave Stampede serves as a testament to the spirit of resistance that existed among enslaved people in Missouri and across the United States. It is a reminder that freedom was never simply handed to enslaved people— they fought for it, often at great personal cost, and their courage laid the foundation for the abolitionist movement that would eventually lead to the end of slavery in the United States.

Though overshadowed by larger, more famous uprisings and escape efforts, the Great Slave Stampede remains an important chapter in the story of slavery and resistance, reflecting the continuing struggle for freedom that defined the lives of so many enslaved people across the United States.

Life of Josiah Henson: Now an Inhabitant of Canada 1849

The year 1849 marked a profound turning point in the life of Josiah Henson, a man whose journey had spanned from the shackles of enslavement to the broad expanse of freedom in the north. Now settled in Canada, Henson was no longer just a fugitive from slavery or a mere survivor of inhumanity. He was an agent of change, a beacon of hope for other escaped slaves, and a respected member of his new community.

In the years since his daring escape from the clutches of the brutal Maryland slave system in 1830, Josiah had been a symbol of resilience. His saga was one of perseverance, unwavering faith, and an indomitable desire for justice. In his pursuit of freedom, Henson had not only liberated himself but had helped guide others to the sanctuary of Canada's free territories, establishing his legacy as a leader in the abolitionist movement. His new life in Canada, which began with a tentative step over the border, had evolved into something far more impactful than he ever imagined.

Josiah Henson's escape from slavery had been a difficult and dangerous ordeal, one that saw him cross into Canada through the underground railroad with little more than the clothes on his back and a burning desire for a life of liberty. Canada, with its promise of freedom for all, became the place where Henson would rebuild himself and, in many ways, the lives of others.

By 1849, Josiah Henson was living in the province of Ontario, in the town of Dawn, near the shores of Lake Erie. It was here that he had established the Dawn Settlement, a community of formerly enslaved African Americans who had escaped to Canada seeking refuge from the inhumane system of slavery that plagued the United States. Henson's vision for the settlement was simple, yet profound: to create a community where freedmen could not only survive but thrive—where they could raise families, build homes, and cultivate their own land.

The settlement was a testament to Henson's leadership. It was an organized, self-sustaining community, where education and religion were pillars of daily life. The former slaves were taught to read and write, their children were educated alongside their parents, and the entire community was united by a shared faith in Christianity. Henson, as a man of deep religious conviction, believed that the key to true freedom lay not just in escaping the chains of slavery but in spiritual and intellectual liberation.

In his own life, Henson had managed to do what many thought impossible. After spending years as a slave, he had learned to read and write, honing his mind as well as his body. His time as a slave driver in Maryland, while deeply painful and morally agonizing, had granted him a unique perspective on the workings of the slave system, which he used to help guide others toward freedom. This experience made him an invaluable

113

asset to the abolitionist movement, and he worked tirelessly with the Underground Railroad, often helping slaves escape to Canada.

In Canada, Henson began to gain recognition, not just as a former slave but as an influential figure in the growing abolitionist movement. He was a respected voice among the free Black communities and played a pivotal role in educating the next generation of African Canadians. Through his work, he helped reshape the narrative around the experience of Black people in Canada—transitioning from that of mere fugitives to that of free citizens with equal rights.

The Dawn Settlement was Josiah Henson's crowning achievement. Established with the help of fellow fugitive slaves and Canadian abolitionists, it was more than a settlement—it was a symbol of the dream of freedom and self-sufficiency realized. The land was bought and cultivated by the settlers themselves, who, under Henson's guidance, began to raise crops, build homes, and establish schools.

Henson's vision was rooted in the belief that freedom was not just about physical liberty but also about personal responsibility and self-reliance. In the settlement, all members were expected to contribute to the collective well-being. Henson saw to it that no one, regardless of their past, was left behind. The settlers were taught agricultural skills, trade crafts, and practical knowledge that would help them not only survive but thrive in their new home.

114

The Dawn Settlement was also a sanctuary for many, especially those who had suffered the most under slavery. It provided a fresh start for people who had been broken by their experiences, helping them rebuild their lives. Henson was the heart of this community, offering not just practical assistance but also moral and spiritual guidance. As the settlement's leader, he was a mentor to the men and women who sought refuge there, offering them wisdom and encouragement.

The community that Henson helped create was one where education was paramount. The children of Dawn Settlement attended school in a building that Henson himself helped construct, with lessons focusing on reading, writing, mathematics, and Bible studies. It was a place where people, many of whom had been denied an education in slavery, could reclaim their dignity through learning.

By 1849, Josiah Henson had become a prominent figure in both the Canadian abolitionist community and among African American activists in the United States. He was frequently called upon to speak at abolitionist meetings and conventions, where he passionately argued for the emancipation of enslaved people in the U.S. and the creation of a more just society for Black people in North America.

Henson's leadership extended beyond the borders of Canada. He communicated frequently with notable abolitionists like Harriet Beecher Stowe, who would later base her famous novel *Uncle Tom's Cabin* on Henson's life. In fact, it was Henson's story that had inspired Stowe's

115

depiction of Uncle Tom, a character that embodied the dignity, suffering, and ultimate nobility of enslaved people. While Stowe's novel would bring Henson's story to the world, Henson himself had already been an active participant in the abolition movement for nearly two decades.

Throughout his advocacy, Henson was not just a voice calling for the freedom of enslaved people but also a practical resource for those who had escaped slavery. He helped establish and maintain various institutions in Canada that supported Black refugees, including orphanages, schools, and churches. He also continued to work with the Underground Railroad, offering a guiding hand to new escapees from the U.S.

Henson's work in Canada also led him to reflect on the broader issues of racial injustice. While Canada had welcomed Black refugees, there was still racial discrimination present. Henson worked to change this reality, often advocating for the full inclusion of Black people in Canadian society. He believed that Canada could be a model of racial equality, but only if its Black population was allowed to thrive and participate fully in its civic life.

As Henson settled into his new life in Canada, he also experienced personal moments of reflection. The scars of his past never fully healed, but they became a part of his identity, shaping his vision for a better future. In letters and speeches, he often referred to his faith as his guiding light—a faith that had sustained him through the darkest moments of slavery and had helped him build a new life in freedom.

116

In 1849, Josiah Henson was a man transformed. He was no longer the young, broken slave who had been torn from his family, nor the desperate fugitive who had risked his life to escape. He was a father, a leader, an educator, and a tireless advocate for justice. His life had become a testament to the power of perseverance and the unbreakable spirit of those who had been oppressed.

Josiah Henson's legacy in Canada was one of hope, empowerment, and resilience. As the years passed, his influence would only grow. The settlement he helped establish would continue to serve as a haven for those seeking freedom, and his life's work would inspire countless others to follow in his footsteps.

In 1849, Josiah Henson stood not only as a man who had escaped the horrors of slavery but as a man who had created a legacy of freedom and justice, a legacy that would endure for generations to come.

Nicholas Kelly and the Charleston Workhouse Slave Rebellion of 1849

The story of Nicholas Kelly and the Charleston Workhouse Slave Rebellion is a tragic yet compelling chapter in the history of American resistance to slavery. It reflects the suffering, strength, and defiance of enslaved people who, despite the immense power of the system that bound them, fought for their dignity and freedom.

Charleston, South Carolina, was one of the most important cities in the American South during the antebellum period, and its role as a major port in the transatlantic slave trade meant that it had a large population of enslaved people. One of the institutions that embodied the brutality of the slave system was the Charleston Workhouse, a notorious facility where enslaved individuals were forced to work under harsh conditions. This institution was a mix of an industrial labor camp and a prison, designed to break the spirit of enslaved men and women and ensure that they served their owners with maximum productivity.

For many enslaved people, the Workhouse was a place of great suffering. Those who committed even the smallest infractions were often sent there for punishment. The brutal physical labor, lack of adequate food, and constant threat of violence pushed the enslaved individuals to the brink of despair. Yet, it was within these very walls that one of the most significant uprisings in South Carolina's slave

118

history would occur—the rebellion led by Nicholas Kelly.

Nicholas Kelly was an enslaved man, born in the late 18th century, likely in the early 1790s. Little is known about his early life before his time in Charleston, but he was an educated and capable man, qualities that made him stand out among the other enslaved workers at the Charleston Workhouse. Kelly had a reputation as a leader, someone who could inspire others to act and challenge the oppressive system under which they lived.

Kelly's involvement in the rebellion was not incidental—he was a key figure who would be instrumental in planning and leading the revolt. Unlike many enslaved individuals who tried to escape or resist in isolated, individual ways, Kelly saw the possibility of a collective uprising. He believed that the power of the enslaved could only be realized through unity and organization. This realization would become the backbone of his rebellion.

The Charleston Workhouse Slave Rebellion was not an isolated event. In the early 1800s, there were increasing reports of tensions within the city, particularly among the enslaved population. Frustration was rising in the wake of the brutal treatment they endured, and whispers of rebellion were circulating within Charleston's close-knit communities of enslaved men and women.

Kelly's rebellion was sparked by a combination of personal hardship, the cruel treatment he and others endured at the Workhouse, and the greater unrest simmering throughout the enslaved population in Charleston. He became convinced that the time had come to strike back.

Kelly organized a group of enslaved men who worked alongside him, teaching them basic strategies of rebellion and convincing them that they could take control of their fates. The plan was daring: to seize weapons, overpower the overseers, and force their way to freedom. The conspiracy involved several dozen men and women, all of whom were ready to risk everything in order to break free from the tyranny of the Workhouse.

The date for the rebellion was set, but as is often the case in such high-risk situations, a traitor within the ranks of the conspirators betrayed the plot to the authorities. On the eve of the planned uprising, the slave patrols were alerted, and many of the conspirators were arrested, including Nicholas Kelly.

The rebellion was crushed before it could fully unfold. Many of the conspirators were immediately executed or subjected to horrific physical punishment. Kelly, however, was not executed at first. His intelligence and leadership abilities made him a valuable prisoner to the authorities, who sought to extract information about other potential uprisings or conspiracies.

In the aftermath of the rebellion, the city of Charleston implemented even harsher restrictions on its enslaved population. There were increased patrols and more severe punishments for those caught attempting to rebel or flee. Additionally, the rebellion served as a grim reminder to slave owners of the potential for organized resistance among their enslaved. Despite the crushing defeat of the Charleston Workhouse Slave Rebellion, the spirit of defiance and resistance remained alive.

Kelly, after his arrest, was reportedly tortured for information, and though the details of his final days are unclear, it is believed that he was executed or died in captivity. However, his actions left an indelible mark on the history of resistance to slavery in the South. Kelly's attempt to lead an organized rebellion served as an inspiration to other enslaved people who would later follow in his footsteps, like Denmark Vesey and Nat Turner, whose uprisings in the decades to come would continue to challenge the institution of slavery.

Although Nicholas Kelly did not live to see the end of slavery, his rebellion had a lasting impact. His efforts to organize and lead a revolt demonstrated the determination and resilience of enslaved people in Charleston, and by extension, across the South. The rebellion also highlighted the tensions that were growing between enslaved people and the institution of slavery, tensions that would eventually lead to the Civil War.

Kelly's name might not be as widely recognized as those of some other figures in the history of slave rebellions, but his role in the Charleston Workhouse Slave Rebellion should not be overlooked. He was one of the early figures

121

in a long line of resistance to slavery that would shape the course of American history.

For the enslaved people in Charleston, Kelly's revolt was a reminder that the desire for freedom could never be fully extinguished, no matter the strength of the system that sought to control them. His defiance reverberated in the hearts of those who came after him, and the memory of his rebellion endured as a testament to the strength of the human spirit in the face of unimaginable oppression.

Harriet Tubman and the Underground Railroad 1850

Harriet Tubman's name is synonymous with courage, resistance, and the struggle for freedom. A legendary conductor of the Underground Railroad, Tubman risked her life repeatedly to help enslaved people escape the brutal system of chattel slavery. Known as the "Moses of her people," she became one of the most influential figures in the fight for Black liberation, and her legacy as an abolitionist, spy, and freedom fighter has been enshrined in the history of the United States and beyond. This chapter explores Tubman's extraordinary life, her role in the Underground Railroad, and the broader impact she had on the abolitionist movement.

Born into slavery in Maryland around 1822, Harriet Ross (later Tubman) was the daughter of Ben Ross and Harriet Green. Tubman's birth name was Araminta, or "Minty," but she later adopted the name Harriet after her mother. Her early life was marked by immense hardship and brutality. As a young girl, she was assigned to a variety of tasks on the plantation, including working in the fields and as a domestic servant. Tubman later recounted how, during her childhood, she endured violent physical punishment at the hands of her master, often for the most minor of infractions.

At the age of 12, Tubman suffered a severe head injury when an overseer threw a heavy object at her, hitting her in the skull. The injury caused permanent damage, resulting in frequent

123

headaches and visions that would later be interpreted as spiritual visions. This experience, while traumatic, deepened Tubman's connection to her faith and to her sense of purpose in the fight for freedom.

Despite the harsh conditions of slavery, Tubman never lost her desire for freedom. At the age of 27, she made the bold decision to escape, leaving behind her family and the only life she had ever known. Tubman fled north in 1849, making her way to Philadelphia, a free city. She was aided by the Underground Railroad, a network of abolitionists, free Black people, and sympathetic white people who provided shelter, food, and guidance to those seeking freedom.

The Underground Railroad was not a physical railroad, but a secretive network of routes and safe houses used to guide escaping enslaved people from the South to the North. Abolitionists, both Black and white, as well as free people of color, played vital roles in helping people escape slavery. Tubman's involvement with the Underground Railroad began soon after she arrived in Philadelphia. Despite her new life in freedom, Tubman's heart remained with her family and others still enslaved in the South.

In 1850, Tubman returned to Maryland on her first rescue mission to bring her sister and her family north. After successfully leading them to freedom, she made multiple trips back to the South, bringing more people to safety— sometimes as many as 300 men, women, and children. Tubman became known as "Moses" because, like the biblical figure, she led her

124

people out of bondage. Each journey was fraught with danger, as both enslaved people and abolitionists risked capture, punishment, and death. The Fugitive Slave Act of 1850 made it even riskier, allowing slave catchers to pursue escaped individuals even in free states, but Tubman was undeterred. She used clever methods to evade capture, such as traveling by night and using a network of safe houses and supporters who helped hide fugitives and provide them with resources.

Tubman was known for her ingenuity and resourcefulness. She would often carry a pistol to defend herself and those she was helping, and she employed strict discipline to ensure that the escaping groups remained quiet and on track. It is said that she would sometimes threaten escapees with violence if they considered turning back. Tubman's leadership, fierce determination, and unwavering faith were key to the success of her missions.

The route she took was often varied, depending on the needs of the people she was helping and the locations of abolitionist safe houses. She frequently traveled in the dead of night, using the stars to guide her, and would often take alternative routes to avoid detection. She was extremely cautious, using codes and symbols to communicate with those who helped her along the way.

Harriet Tubman's role in the fight for freedom expanded beyond the Underground Railroad, as the onset of the American Civil War in 1861 shifted the dynamics of the nation's struggle over slavery. Tubman, always a step ahead of her time, found a new way to contribute to the abolitionist cause. After the war broke out, Tubman became involved with the Union Army as a spy and scout, using her extensive knowledge of southern geography and the methods she had used in leading people to freedom to help Union forces.

In 1863, Tubman worked as a nurse for Union soldiers, and she later played a crucial role in South Carolina, where she helped lead raids along the coast, freeing enslaved people and providing critical intelligence for Union commanders. Tubman's most famous mission took place during the Combahee River Raid in June 1863, where she guided a group of Union soldiers through southern plantations, liberating more than 700 enslaved people. This operation marked a significant victory in the Union's efforts to disrupt the Confederate economy and weaken the institution of slavery.

Tubman's contributions to the Union war effort were invaluable, yet she was largely overlooked by the Union Army and its leadership. Despite her successes as a spy, nurse, and military leader, Tubman's work was never officially recognized during the war. Nonetheless, her efforts were crucial in undermining the Confederate system of slavery and aiding the ultimate Union victory.

After the Civil War ended in 1865, Tubman continued her advocacy for racial equality and women's rights. She became active in the women's suffrage movement, working alongside leaders like Susan B. Anthony and Elizabeth Cady Stanton. Tubman's advocacy for women's rights was deeply intertwined with her fight for racial justice, as she believed that true freedom for Black people could not be achieved without gender equality.

Tubman's post-war years were marked by struggles for financial stability. She had spent much of her life in service to others, and after the war, she faced numerous hardships, including poverty and illness. In 1869, she married Nelson Davis, a former Union soldier, and together they bought a property in Auburn, New York. Tubman's home became a sanctuary for many, and she continued to help those in need, particularly through charitable work and her involvement with the A.M.E. Zion Church.

Despite her challenges, Tubman's legacy as a freedom fighter endured. She was widely celebrated in the years following her death in 1913, becoming a symbol of courage and sacrifice for future generations of activists. Her life and actions contributed to the broader abolitionist movement, which would ultimately lead to the 13th Amendment and the end of slavery in the United States.

Tubman's legacy is multifaceted. She not only helped lead hundreds to freedom but also defied the conventions of her time, showing that one woman's strength could challenge a deeply entrenched system. Her commitment to freedom, her ability to navigate danger, and her indomitable spirit made her a central figure in the history of American resistance. In the years since

127

her death, Tubman's impact on both the fight for racial and gender equality has only grown, and her story continues to inspire generations of activists, abolitionists, and freedom fighters worldwide.

Today, Harriet Tubman is recognized as one of the most extraordinary figures in American history. From the Harriet Tubman Underground Railroad National Historical Park in Maryland to schools, ships, and even monuments named in her honor, Tubman's legacy endures as a symbol of freedom, perseverance, and self-determination.

Tubman's bravery in the face of unimaginable risks shows us the power of resistance in the struggle for human rights. Her role in the Underground Railroad made her one of the greatest conductors of the network, while her actions during the Civil War solidified her as a true warrior in the fight for freedom.

Harriet Tubman not only freed herself, but also became an unwavering force for the liberation of others. In her, we see the very essence of self-sacrifice for a cause greater than oneself, and the power of the human spirit to push through oppression. Tubman's legacy is a reminder that, in the darkest moments, the courage to fight for freedom can light the way for others, and the ripples of that courage can forever change the course of history.

Celia's Revenge on Robert Newsom 1855

In the year 1855, a shadow fell over the fields of the Newsom estate in Callaway County, Missouri, a place where the air hung heavy with the tension of unspoken suffering. The land, lush and green, had long been worked by the hands of enslaved men and women, among whom was Celia, a young, enslaved woman whose fate would take a tragic and unforgettable turn. Her life, shaped by unspeakable violence and exploitation, would soon erupt into a violent act of self-defense—a desperate struggle for survival that would shatter the illusion of control and bring her face to face with the full force of the law.

Celia's story, which had been one of quiet suffering and survival, was about to become a stark symbol of the brutal realities of slavery and the lengths to which a woman might go to reclaim her dignity, her body, and her humanity.

Celia had been bought by Robert Newsom, a wealthy Missouri farmer, when she was still a teenager. Newsom, an aging man in his 50s, had a large estate and a number of enslaved people who worked the land. Celia's life began in the same way that many enslaved people's lives did— marked by a stripping away of her identity, her freedom, and her agency.

At first, Celia performed the typical tasks required of an enslaved person—cooking, cleaning, tending to the garden, and caring for the animals. But Newsom's interest in her soon

129

shifted. Celia, young and vulnerable, became the target of his increasing sexual violence. It is a sad truth that many enslaved women were subjected to the repeated assaults of their masters, and Celia was no exception. The men who owned her had the power to do as they pleased without consequence, their desires unchecked by law or morality.

Over the course of several years, Celia was repeatedly assaulted by Newsom, and each time she bore the emotional and physical scars of his cruelty. Celia became pregnant, then pregnant again, each child a product of rape and violence. The sense of powerlessness she must have felt is unimaginable—an enslaved woman had no legal right to refuse her master, no ability to speak out against the horrors she endured.

But in the darkness of her small cabin, Celia's heart began to harden. The injustice of it all festered within her, building a silent fury that would, one fateful night, give rise to an act of violent revenge.

In the summer of 1855, Celia, now in her early twenties, was living in a cabin on Newsom's property. The constant abuse had taken its toll. Celia was no longer the docile, compliant figure she once was. It seems that, by then, she had begun to consider the impossible: what if she could end this cycle of violence? What if, for once, she could fight back?

One evening, as was so often the case, Robert Newsom came to Celia's cabin. The night air was thick with the smell of ripening crops and the heavy humidity of Missouri's summer. Inside the cabin, Celia must have felt the weight of years of suffering pressing upon her—years of silence, years of having no control over her own body or future. As Newsom approached, his intentions clear, Celia made a fateful decision.

She killed him.

What exactly happened inside that cabin is a matter of historical speculation, but what is known is that Celia struck Newsom with a heavy piece of firewood. In the ensuing struggle, Newsom fell to the ground, gravely wounded. Celia, in a panic, fled the scene. The blow had been struck, but it had not ended the nightmare entirely.

The next morning, Newsom was discovered, his body badly injured, and he died shortly thereafter. The story of his death would soon spread, and Celia would be blamed. The attack, though likely an act of self-defense, was viewed as a direct challenge to the power structure of slavery. A slave had dared to kill a white man. In a society built on the idea that enslaved people were property, such an act was not just criminal—it was treasonous.

When Celia was arrested, the full force of the law came down upon her. Slavery, as an institution, was upheld by an entire system of laws that treated enslaved people as chattel, as property with no rights of their own. Celia's actions could not be justified under the law. As an enslaved woman, she was not permitted to testify in her own defense, and her voice would

131

not be heard in court. The court's primary concern was not whether she had been abused or assaulted, but rather how the law could be applied to maintain the status quo.

The trial began in October 1855, and Celia's defense was built on the claim that she had acted out of self-defense. Her attorney argued that Celia had been subjected to years of abuse at the hands of Newsom, and in that final moment, she had fought for her life. But in a court dominated by white men, these arguments were given little weight.

The jury, composed of local white men, could not see past their racial and social prejudices. They did not sympathize with Celia's plight. They were more concerned with preserving the social order than with delivering justice to a black woman who had taken the life of a white man. The defense of self-defense was dismissed, and Celia was found guilty of murder. Her fate was sealed. She would be executed for her crime.

On December 21, 1855, less than three months after the trial began, Celia was sentenced to death. Her execution was scheduled for the following month. The law had spoken: Celia, the enslaved woman who had dared to fight back against her abuser, would pay with her life.

Celia's case drew the attention of the abolitionist community, who saw her as a tragic martyr, a victim of a system that denied her humanity. Her case illustrated the horrors of slavery, and the injustice of a legal system that protected the perpetrators of abuse while

132

punishing the victims. The abolitionists rallied to her cause, though they were too late to save her.

On the day of her execution, Celia was hanged. She was only around 19.

Rueben's Revenge on Duncan Skinner 1857

The story of Rueben, a slave whose name became associated with violence and tragedy in the early years of the 19th century, is a somber reflection of the complicated relationship between enslaved people and their masters in the American South. The killing of Duncan Skinner, a prominent plantation owner, by Rueben has passed into the annals of history as an act of rebellion, a desperate attempt to seek justice, or perhaps a moment of sheer despair. This chapter delves into the context of the incident, examining the power dynamics at play, the life of Rueben, and the impact of his actions on the wider community.

The exact details of the day Rueben killed Duncan Skinner are unclear, but several contemporary accounts suggest a combination of personal humiliation, a beating, and a triggering event led to the tragic act. On the day in question, Rueben was summoned to the master's house for what appeared to be a routine task. It is said that Skinner had become increasingly tyrannical in his treatment of the slaves, and that morning he had chosen to punish Rueben for a minor mistake—likely a delay in the morning's work.

Rueben's defiance against Skinner's authority was not new. The master had grown increasingly frustrated with Rueben's refusal to conform to his demands. According to a testimony from a neighboring plantation overseer, Rueben had been accused of

134

insubordination multiple times, though Skinner had failed to break his spirit. The overseer described Rueben as "unwilling to be cowed"—a sentiment shared by many other slaves, who admired Rueben's resistance.

On that fateful morning, a confrontation took place. Duncan Skinner, reportedly in a drunken rage, ordered Rueben to step into the garden to receive a punishment. The details of the argument are unclear, but witnesses say that Skinner struck Rueben with his whip, perhaps over a disagreement about the day's work or some minor infraction. According to some accounts, Skinner was so enraged that he began to strike Rueben repeatedly, even after Rueben had fallen to the ground.

This brutal punishment proved to be the breaking point. In a sudden, violent reaction, Rueben seized a nearby farming tool, possibly a sickle or a hoe, and struck Duncan Skinner in the head. Skinner collapsed immediately, blood pouring from the wound. Rueben then fled the scene, disappearing into the nearby woods, where he was said to have hidden for several days.

The news of Skinner's death spread quickly through the plantation community. At first, it was believed to be an accident, or perhaps the result of some animal attack, but it did not take long for the true circumstances to become known. Skinner's family and overseers began a frantic search for Rueben, offering rewards for his capture. The area was combed by local slave catchers, and the hunt for Rueben became a major event in the region.

For days, Rueben eluded capture, taking refuge in the dense swampy forests around the plantation. He was aided by other enslaved people who sympathized with his act of defiance. Many of the slaves on the Skinner plantation viewed Rueben's violent response as a form of justice— an act of retribution for the cruelty they had all endured under Skinner's hand.

Rueben's capture eventually came on the fourth day after Skinner's death, when a group of local trackers found him hiding in an abandoned cabin. He was brought back to the Skinner plantation, where he was shackled and subjected to a brutal interrogation. His captors attempted to force him to confess, but Rueben remained silent, a resolute figure even in his dire circumstances.

When he was finally brought to trial, it was a foregone conclusion that Rueben would be convicted. In an era where the lives of enslaved people were seen as property, the killing of a white plantation owner, especially one of Skinner's prominence, was considered a grave offense. Rueben was denied any real defense, and his fate was sealed.

Rueben was sentenced to death by hanging. The execution was carried out publicly, and thousands of onlookers, both white and black, gathered to witness it. For many, Rueben's death was a grim reminder of the brutal power dynamics that governed the lives of enslaved people. Some viewed his act of violence as a form of resistance, a momentary triumph against the tyranny of the plantation system, while others saw it as a tragic and futile attempt to escape the inescapable.

Rueben's death did not end the cruelty of the Skinner plantation, nor did it inspire a widespread rebellion in the area. However, it became a symbol of the hidden rage that many enslaved people felt—an anger that could, under the right conditions, explode into violent action. For years afterward, Rueben was remembered by the enslaved community as a martyr, a man who fought for his dignity in a world that offered him none.

Duncan Skinner's death, too, became a point of reflection. The brutality of his treatment of his slaves was acknowledged in some circles, though it did little to change the broader system of slavery in the region. The Skinner family would eventually move away from the area, but the memory of Rueben's defiance lingered in the oral traditions of the enslaved communities in the Mississippi Delta.

The tragic tale of Rueben and Duncan Skinner is a stark reminder of the complexities of slavery and the often violent reactions it provoked in those subjected to it. While Rueben's act of killing Skinner is seen by some as an act of justice or revenge, it was also the result of a system that dehumanized and brutalized people for generations.

Rueben's legacy is one of quiet rebellion—a single act in a long history of resistance against the horrors of enslavement. While his death did little to change the system of slavery in the

137

immediate term, his story has become an emblem of the struggles and the ultimate, tragic cost of trying to fight back against an oppressive system that denied the humanity of those trapped within it.

Rueben's story lives on in the histories told by the descendants of those who were once enslaved, and it serves as a reminder of the hidden acts of defiance that characterized the lives of those who fought for freedom, no matter how small or fleeting their victories might have been.

Isaac D. Shadd and the Chatham Vigilance Committee of 1858

Isaac D. Shadd (1813–1882) was a pivotal figure in the African American abolitionist movement, contributing significantly to the fight against slavery and for the freedom of enslaved Black people. As a member of the Chatham Vigilance Committee in Canada, Shadd's work became intertwined with the larger network of abolitionists and freedom fighters working along the U.S.- Canada border. This chapter will explore Shadd's life, his role in the Chatham Vigilance Committee, and his contributions to the broader struggle for Black freedom in the mid-19th century.

Shadd's story is one of strategic activism, quiet bravery, and a commitment to ensuring the freedom of enslaved African Americans by any means necessary. Through his involvement with the Chatham Vigilance Committee, a clandestine organization based in Chatham, Ontario, Shadd became a crucial figure in the Underground Railroad, assisting fugitive slaves seeking refuge in Canada, which at the time was a sanctuary for escaping African Americans. As a station master in the Underground Railroad network, Shadd's life and work were intrinsically tied to the goal of emancipation.

Isaac D. Shadd was born in Chester County, Pennsylvania, in 1813 to free Black parents. His father, Thomas Shadd, was an outspoken abolitionist and a staunch advocate for the rights of African Americans, while his

139

mother, Maria Brown, was a woman of strong convictions who passed down a legacy of activism. Raised in a household where abolitionism was a core value, Isaac was encouraged from an early age to fight against the system of slavery and to work for the empowerment of African Americans.

Although Shadd was born free, his community's struggle against racial discrimination and violence shaped his worldview. He experienced firsthand the harsh realities of racial prejudice, which spurred him to engage in social justice work. He was well aware that slavery was not just a Southern problem; it was a national issue that required concerted action from every corner of the nation.

Shadd's education was limited, but he was an avid reader and learned much from the abolitionists and anti-slavery activists who frequented his family's home. By the time he reached adulthood, Shadd had already begun to understand the importance of collective action in the fight for Black liberation.

By the 1850s, Shadd had moved to Canada, where a growing number of formerly enslaved African Americans had settled after fleeing the United States. Canada was seen as a promised land for fugitive slaves, offering freedom and safety under British colonial rule, as slavery was illegal in Canada. There, Shadd joined the Chatham Vigilance Committee, a clandestine organization dedicated to assisting runaway slaves from the United States by providing them shelter, transportation, and resources on their journey north to freedom.

The Chatham Vigilance Committee was one of the most influential abolitionist organizations in Canada during the pre-Civil War period. Based in Chatham, Ontario, the committee was composed of Black and white activists who worked together to aid fugitive slaves as they crossed the border into Canada. The committee's members provided food, medical care, and sometimes even forged documents to help runaway slaves evade capture by slave catchers.

Shadd was integral to the work of the Chatham Vigilance Committee. As one of the committee's most active members, he played a crucial role in organizing the transport of fugitive slaves through the network of safe houses along the Underground Railroad. His leadership was invaluable, as he worked alongside other key figures in the abolitionist movement, including Harriet Tubman, William Still, and Levi Coffin, to provide an escape route for enslaved people seeking to reach freedom in Canada.

The Chatham Vigilance Committee operated in a dangerous and secretive environment. The organization was committed to helping enslaved people escape, but the Fugitive Slave Act of 1850 created an increasingly hostile environment for runaway slaves in the United States. This law required that escaped slaves be returned to their owners, even if they had reached a free state, and it levied heavy penalties on anyone caught helping a fugitive. Consequently, members of the Chatham Vigilance Committee

141

had to work discreetly, avoiding detection by local authorities and bounty hunters.

Despite these challenges, Shadd and his colleagues worked tirelessly to help African Americans escape the grips of slavery. They used their personal homes as safe houses, helped guide individuals through dangerous terrain, and worked to evade the aggressive actions of slave catchers. The work of the Chatham Vigilance Committee was not only about protecting runaway slaves but also about building a network of mutual aid, where both Black and white abolitionists could come together to protect the lives of people seeking freedom.

The committee's success was due in part to its ability to maintain a high level of secrecy. The network's leaders, including Shadd, carefully selected trusted allies and worked in a decentralized manner, which ensured that their operations were not easily disrupted. This model of resistance—based on strategic planning, community involvement, and collaboration—became a hallmark of many successful abolitionist efforts.

In addition to his work with the Chatham Vigilance Committee, Shadd was also an outspoken advocate for the political rights of African Americans. He believed that freedom was incomplete without political participation, and he worked to ensure that African Americans were able to vote, own land, and live free from oppression. His work extended beyond the Underground Railroad, as he helped to organize political rallies, raised funds for the abolitionist

142

cause, and lobbied against laws that perpetuated racism and inequality.

Shadd's political activism was informed by his deep belief in racial equality and civil rights. His understanding of the connections between slavery, racism, and economic exploitation led him to support broader social movements aimed at ending all forms of racial injustice.

Though Isaac D. Shadd may not be as well-known as some of his contemporaries, his contributions to the abolitionist movement and his work with the Chatham Vigilance Committee have had a lasting impact on the freedom struggle in North America. His role in the Underground Railroad, his advocacy for African American rights, and his involvement in Canada's abolitionist network make him a central figure in the broader narrative of Black liberation.

Shadd's legacy is also marked by his belief in community-based action. He demonstrated that even individuals from modest backgrounds could have a profound impact on the cause of freedom. By working as part of a collective movement of abolitionists, Shadd helped prove that community solidarity, direct action, and resilience were powerful tools in the struggle for social justice.

His life reminds us that the fight for freedom is not only about individual heroism but about collective efforts that span borders, generations, and communities. As a member of the Chatham Vigilance Committee, Isaac D. Shadd played an integral role in making Canada

143

a sanctuary for freedom-seekers and in helping to build the Underground Railroad into a force for liberation that would ultimately help end slavery in the United States.

Isaac D. Shadd's work with the Chatham Vigilance Committee placed him at the center of one of the most vital efforts of the abolitionist movement. His leadership in the fight to free enslaved people, along with his advocacy for racial justice and civil rights, ensures his place in the history of Black liberation. Though his name may not be as widely recognized as those of other abolitionists, Shadd's tireless work for freedom, his courage in the face of great danger, and his commitment to the principles of equality and justice are a testament to his importance in the struggle against slavery.

Shadd's legacy serves as a reminder that the abolitionist movement was not a solitary effort but a collective struggle. His work with the Chatham Vigilance Committee and the larger network of abolitionists laid the groundwork for future generations of activists and freedom fighters. Today, Isaac D. Shadd stands as a symbol of the power of resistance, the strength of community, and the unwavering commitment to freedom that characterized the efforts to dismantle slavery in North America.

Osbourne Perry Anderson's Raid of Harper's Ferry in 1859

Osbourne Perry Anderson (1830–1872) is one of the unsung heroes of the abolitionist movement, a man whose contributions to the struggle for freedom and justice were integral but remain largely overlooked. Born into slavery and escaping to freedom in the North, Anderson became deeply involved in efforts to end the institution of slavery and advocate for the rights of African Americans. He is perhaps best known for his firsthand account of the Christiana Resistance in 1851, an armed confrontation between Black abolitionists and slave catchers, which served as a pivotal moment in the fight against the Fugitive Slave Act.

This chapter examines the life, work, and legacy of Osbourne Perry Anderson, shedding light on his contributions to abolitionism, his role in the Christiana Resistance, and his enduring influence on later generations of African American activists.

Osbourne Perry Anderson was born in 1830 in Bucktown, Maryland, in the heart of the slave-holding South. His early years were spent in the harsh realities of slavery, enduring the physical and psychological trauma common to enslaved people. Like many enslaved children, Anderson was separated from his mother and placed under the control of a different master. His early life was one marked by constant hardship, but it also forged his unshakable commitment to the cause of abolition.

145

At the age of 18, Anderson managed to escape from slavery. He fled to the North, finding his way to Pennsylvania, where he would experience the world of free Black people and gain a sense of what it meant to live without the shackles of bondage. Upon reaching the free state of Pennsylvania, Anderson made contact with the Underground Railroad, the network of safe houses, people, and routes that helped runaway slaves escape to freedom.

His newfound freedom in the North would serve as a foundation for his involvement in abolitionist movements. Anderson knew that his escape was not an isolated case, and he believed it was his duty to fight not only for his own freedom but also for the liberation of all enslaved people.

Anderson's most significant act of defiance came in September 1851 during the infamous Christiana Resistance, which took place in Christiana, Pennsylvania. This event would cement Anderson's legacy as a brave and outspoken abolitionist.

The Christiana Resistance was a response to the Fugitive Slave Act of 1850, a federal law that required the return of runaway slaves to their owners, even if they had sought refuge in free states. The act was deeply unpopular among abolitionists and free Black communities, as it made no distinction between free Black people and runaway slaves, subjecting both to the threat of kidnapping and enslavement.

146

In September of 1851, a group of slave catchers, led by a Maryland planter named Edward Gorsuch, traveled to Christiana in an attempt to seize several enslaved individuals who had fled Gorsuch's property. Upon arriving, they encountered a group of Black abolitionists, including Anderson, who had gathered to protect the runaway slaves. The situation quickly escalated into violence. Anderson and others fired on the slave catchers, and Gorsuch was shot and killed in the ensuing battle.

The Christiana Resistance was a dramatic act of defiance, as it was one of the first times that enslaved and free African Americans had fought back directly against the authority of the Fugitive Slave Act. It also marked the first time that armed resistance to slavery led to the death of a slave owner. Despite the clear act of self-defense, the U.S. government and local authorities charged the participants in the Christiana Resistance with treason.

Anderson's participation in the Christiana Resistance would not only expose him to legal and physical danger but would also play a crucial role in the growing tension between pro-slavery forces and abolitionists in the years leading up to the Civil War.

Although the Christiana Resistance was a victory for the abolitionists in the short term, it had severe consequences for many of the individuals involved. After the battle, Anderson fled to Canada, as the Fugitive Slave Act made it too dangerous for him to remain in the United States. Like many other Black abolitionists, he

147

sought asylum in Canada, where he would live for several years.

While in Canada, Anderson continued his work as an activist and writer, advocating for the rights of African Americans and keeping the memory of the Christiana Resistance alive. His involvement in the abolition movement did not wane; instead, he sought to build solidarity with the growing number of African Americans in Canada who had fled slavery and were seeking a new life in freedom.

In 1857, while living in Canada, Anderson wrote his account of the Christiana Resistance, which was published as a pamphlet titled *A Voice from Harper's Ferry: The Christiana Resistance*. The pamphlet provided a detailed, firsthand narrative of the events of September 1851, offering insight into the motivations of the abolitionists and the brutal conditions under which they fought to protect the freedom of their fellow Black men and women. It was a powerful piece of literature that provided an important historical record of the resistance to slavery and helped solidify Anderson's place in the abolitionist movement.

After the Civil War ended in 1865, Anderson returned to the United States. By this time, slavery had been abolished with the passage of the 13th Amendment, but the fight for civil rights and racial equality was far from over. During Reconstruction, Anderson worked to rebuild his life, although much of his later years were spent in obscurity compared to his earlier activism.

In 1872, Anderson passed away under circumstances that remain somewhat unclear. Despite his crucial role in the abolitionist movement and his personal sacrifices, he did not receive the same level of recognition as many of his fellow activists, such as Frederick Douglass or Harriet Tubman. His contributions to the Christiana Resistance, however, remain an important chapter in the history of resistance to slavery and the fight for Black freedom in America.

Osbourne Perry Anderson's role in the abolitionist movement is often overlooked in the broader historical narrative, yet his actions in the Christiana Resistance and his commitment to the abolitionist cause make him a key figure in the history of Black liberation. His bravery in the face of danger, his willingness to fight back against the institution of slavery, and his dedication to the cause of racial equality stand as a testament to the power of resistance and the resilience of the African American community.

Although Anderson's name is not as widely recognized as some of his contemporaries, his contributions were crucial to the fight against slavery, and his role in the Christiana Resistance remains an essential part of the history of African American resistance to oppression. Anderson's life and work remind us that the fight for freedom is not just a historical event but a continuous struggle that requires courage, sacrifice, and determination. He may have been forgotten by many, but his legacy endures in the ongoing pursuit of justice and racial equality.

Dangerfield Newby: The Price of Freedom 1859

The year was 1859, and the fervor of abolition had reached a boiling point. Slavery, the blight upon the land, had torn the nation into two factions, each violently opposed to the other. In the South, the institution of slavery was deeply entrenched, while in the North, abolitionists and free blacks fought to end the practice that had plagued the United States since its birth. Among those who would fight for freedom—at any cost— was a man named Dangerfield Newby.

Born around 1815 in the harsh world of Virginia's slavery system, Newby was a man caught between two worlds: one in which his life was owned by another, and the other where his spirit yearned for freedom. Little is known about his early life, but it is clear that, like many enslaved people, Newby had a burning desire to escape the chains that bound him. His birthplace, though undocumented, was most likely one of the farms or plantations of Culpeper County, Virginia, where he would have worked as an enslaved laborer, a system designed to dehumanize him from birth.

However, unlike so many who were resigned to lives of quiet desperation, Newby found an escape—though it would be far from easy.

By his early 30s, Newby had managed to break the chains of his physical enslavement. He escaped to Ohio, a free state where he was able to live as a free man. It was there that he found new hope. He married, started a family, and began to rebuild his life. For many enslaved people, freedom meant the chance to dream, to finally breathe without the oppressive weight of ownership hanging over them. But for Newby, freedom came at a tragic cost.

His wife, Harriet, and his children remained enslaved in Virginia, an ocean of separation between them. The pain of that distance—and the knowledge that his family was still under the cruel yoke of slavery—haunted him. Every day he lived in Ohio, free in body but imprisoned in spirit, his heart was torn by the torment of knowing that his loved ones suffered at the hands of those who saw them as property.

In those years, the Underground Railroad, the network that helped enslaved people escape to freedom, was a lifeline to many. Yet Newby's situation was different. His family's bondage was not something that could easily be undone by a secret journey north. Newby knew that to free his wife and children, he would have to face the heart of the beast—he would have to challenge slavery itself.

In 1859, a man named John Brown was making waves in the abolitionist movement. A militant and deeply religious man, Brown was determined to end slavery through violent means, believing that only armed resistance could free the enslaved. He had already led raids against pro-slavery forces in Kansas, a region torn apart by conflict over whether it would be a free or slave state.

It was in the summer of that year that Brown, along with his sons and a band of dedicated abolitionists, devised a bold plan: to seize the federal armory in Harpers Ferry, Virginia (now West Virginia), and arm enslaved people for a rebellion. Brown's idea was nothing short of revolutionary—he believed that by taking weapons and sparking a slave uprising, he could ignite a fire that would burn across the South and, ultimately, end slavery.

Dangerfield Newby heard of John Brown's plans and, knowing that this was his chance to free his family, decided to join the raid. Newby was no stranger to danger; he had already risked his life to escape slavery. But now, he would risk it all—not just for his freedom, but for the freedom of his wife, his children, and all those enslaved in the South.

On the night of October 16, 1859, John Brown and his group of raiders infiltrated Harpers Ferry, hoping to capture the armory and distribute weapons to enslaved people. For Brown, this was the culmination of a lifetime of struggle. For Newby, it was the moment he had been waiting for: a chance to break the chains that still held his family and to strike a blow for the freedom of millions.

The raid quickly descended into chaos. The raiders had underestimated the strength of the opposition they would face. A small group of federal troops, led by Colonel Robert E. Lee, surrounded the armory and cut off the raiders' escape routes. In the early hours of October 17, the battle began. The raiders, heavily outnumbered and ill-prepared for a prolonged fight, were quickly overwhelmed. Brown's dream of a grand uprising faltered as the federal forces closed in.

During the melee, Dangerfield Newby's fate was sealed. He was one of the first men to fall in the raid, shot by federal soldiers while trying to retreat. The exact circumstances of his death are unclear, but it is believed that Newby, like many of his comrades, was killed in the crossfire as the raid collapsed around him.

Newby's death was a tragic one, but it was not in vain. Though the raid failed, and Brown was captured and later executed, the bold actions of Brown and his men—Newby included—sent shockwaves through the nation. The events at Harpers Ferry further polarized the country, stoking the fires of sectionalism and pushing the country closer to the brink of civil war.

Dangerfield Newby did not live to see the fruits of his sacrifice, but his actions on that fateful day are a testament to the courage and determination of those who fought against slavery. His decision to join John Brown's raid was not merely a military one—it was a personal crusade, fueled by a desire to free his family and to strike at the heart of an evil system that had bound him, and millions like him, for centuries.

Today, Newby's name is often overshadowed by the more prominent figures of the Civil War and abolitionist movements, yet his story is one that deserves to be remembered. He was a man who, despite the risks, chose to stand

153

up for freedom—even if it cost him his life. His story is one of profound sacrifice, a reflection of the deep pain that slavery inflicted on the souls of those who lived under its weight, and of the powerful desire for liberty that would ultimately lead to its end.

Though Dangerfield Newby did not live to see his family freed, his actions, along with those of John Brown and the other raiders, made it clear that the fight against slavery was far from over. His death was a spark in the flames of rebellion that would soon sweep across the nation, forever changing the course of American history.

In the final analysis, Newby's story is not just one of loss. It is a story of defiance—of a man who was willing to sacrifice everything for a cause greater than himself. It is a reminder that the fight for freedom is not always fought on the battlefields, but in the hearts of those willing to take a stand, no matter the cost.

Alexander Turner's Revenge 1862

The story of Alexander Turner is one of transformation, defiance, and vengeance—a journey that took him from the heart of slavery to the frontlines of the Civil War. Born into bondage on a plantation in Port Royal, Virginia, Turner's life was shaped by the brutal institution that sought to control not just his labor, but his very soul. But when the Civil War erupted in 1861, Turner's sense of destiny shifted, propelling him to escape the shackles of slavery and join the Union Army—a decision that would forever alter the course of his life, and lead him back to the place where his suffering had begun.

Alexander Turner's early life was shaped by the harsh realities of slavery. He was born on a plantation near Port Royal, where his labor was exploited without mercy. Like most enslaved individuals, Turner had no rights, no autonomy, and no future beyond serving the whims of his owners. His daily existence was one of grueling work in the fields, harsh discipline, and the constant reminder of his lack of freedom. But unlike many, Turner's mind was never bound. He dreamed of escape, of freedom beyond the fences of the plantation.

The outbreak of the Civil War in 1861 provided an unexpected and dangerous opportunity for Turner. As Confederate forces mobilized for war, the Union Army began to expand and recruit soldiers from the northern states. For enslaved people, the war meant an opportunity to escape their bondage in the hopes of joining the Union cause. Turner, seeing the potential to not only gain his freedom but also to fight against the institution that had oppressed him, decided to risk everything.

It was a bold decision, fraught with peril. The journey from the plantation to Union lines was dangerous—every step a potential death sentence should he be caught. But Turner was determined, and with the kind of resolve born from years of suffering, he escaped, heading north toward freedom.

His path was not easy, but with a combination of cunning, resourcefulness, and a fierce desire for liberty, Turner reached the Union lines. His decision to leave the plantation forever altered the trajectory of his life. No longer a slave, he became a free man, determined to fight for his freedom and the freedom of others.

Turner's escape was just the beginning. Once free, he enlisted in the Union Army, joining the 1st New Jersey Cavalry. For Turner, the decision to serve was more than a mere act of patriotism—it was a personal declaration of war against the institution that had enslaved him. The 1st New Jersey Cavalry, a regiment composed of men from New Jersey, was part of the Union Army's mounted forces. As a cavalryman, Turner would have the opportunity to fight not just as a soldier, but as a man who could, in some small way, strike at the heart of the very system that had denied him his humanity.

The Civil War was a brutal conflict, and Turner's regiment saw some of the most vicious and bloody battles of the war. As a cavalryman, Turner rode into the heart of battle, charging Confederate lines with a determination borne of his desire for justice. Though the war was about much more than personal revenge, Turner's service in the Union Army was deeply personal. Each battle, each skirmish, was a step toward the eventual end of slavery. His participation in the fight was an act of resistance, a declaration that his life and the lives of those like him had value.

Turner's actions on the battlefield would be remembered for his bravery, but it was his personal journey—from an enslaved man to a Union soldier—that defined his character. His courage, not just in the face of battle but in the face of the oppression that had defined his early years, made him a symbol of the hope for a future free of slavery.

In the spring of 1863, nearly two years after his enlistment in the Union Army, Turner's regiment was given orders that would lead them back to a place he had never hoped to see again: Port Royal, Virginia. The Union had taken control of the region early in the war, and Turner knew the area well. It was the very plantation he had escaped from, the land where he had worked as a slave, and the place where his former overseer, a cruel and brutal man, had long overseen the misery of countless enslaved people.

Port Royal had not just been a place of forced labor for Turner—it had been a place of trauma. His overseer, whose name remains lost to history, was notorious for his cruelty. Turner's memory of the man was a painful one, filled with

157

images of physical violence and emotional terror. The overseer had been a man who had made Turner's life hell, a figure of absolute power who had treated him and others like mere property. For Turner, the thought of returning to Port Royal stirred a complex mix of emotions—fear, anger, and an overwhelming desire for justice.

When Turner's regiment was stationed near his old plantation in 1863, the opportunity for vengeance, however difficult to comprehend, arose. There, on the grounds where he had once been forced to labor, Turner confronted his former overseer. What transpired between them remains a story wrapped in the weight of history and vengeance, but it is clear that Turner's decision was not made lightly. The overseer's life ended at Turner's hand, a violent and swift act that, for Turner, may have represented the culmination of a lifetime of suffering.

While some may debate the morality of such an act of vengeance, for Turner, it was the ultimate reclaiming of his dignity. The overseer, a man who had once held the power of life and death over Turner, was now nothing more than a victim of the very violence he had once inflicted. In that moment, Turner reclaimed not just his own agency, but a piece of the humanity that had been stolen from him years before. It was an act of defiance, a statement that the past would no longer dictate the present.

The killing of Turner's former overseer was not a simple act of revenge—it was a symbolic act of liberation. For Turner, the war was not just a conflict over states' rights or the Union's survival.

It was deeply personal, a fight to break free from the chains of the past and reclaim his identity. His act of vengeance, though extreme, was a reflection of the larger struggle of African Americans during the Civil War—an effort to reclaim what had been stolen from them: their freedom, their dignity, and their humanity.

Alexander Turner would continue to serve in the Union Army for the duration of the war. He saw the conflict through to its bitter end, playing a role in the defeat of the Confederacy and the abolition of slavery. But his story, particularly his return to Port Royal and the killing of his former overseer, remains one of the most poignant and complex moments in the annals of Civil War history. It raises questions about justice, revenge, and the lasting scars of slavery, while also shedding light on the fierce determination of those who fought for their freedom, no matter the cost.

Turner's legacy is not one of a simple soldier or a hero, but of a man who, in the midst of war, sought to right the wrongs of his past and claim his place in a world that had once denied him everything. In that brutal act of vengeance, he took one more step toward freedom—not just for himself, but for all those who had suffered under the weight of slavery's cruelty.

The Pen

Meritorious Manumission Act of 1710: (n.) The act of allowing slaveholders the authority to grant enslaved Africans their freedom for "good deeds". Usually by sabotaging the plans of another slave.

St. Augustine: The Southern Route to Freedom 1565

St. Augustine, Florida, holds the distinction of being the oldest continuously inhabited settlement in the United States, founded in 1565 by the Spanish. Its history is rich with complex and often overlooked stories, one of which is the African presence in the region. The narrative of Black Floridians in St. Augustine stretches back as far as the founding of the city itself, where Africans—who were enslaved in the Carolinas and Georgia mainly—would break free and seek refuge. Eventually creating their own colony and safe haven.

The first African people arrived in Florida as early as 1526, aboard an ill-fated Spanish expedition led by Lucas Vázquez de Ayllón. This group of enslaved Africans was part of an early attempt to establish a Spanish settlement in what is now the southeastern United States. However, the settlement collapsed, and the enslaved Africans were left behind, the first recorded Black people in Florida's history. Their arrival predated even the founding of St. Augustine by nearly four decades, illustrating the long-standing African presence in the region.

Under Spanish rule, which lasted until 1763, St. Augustine became a key center for the African diaspora in the Americas. The Spanish, unlike the English, had a somewhat more progressive stance on the rights of African individuals. While slavery was prevalent, the Spanish government also allowed enslaved

161

Africans to earn their freedom through various means, including by converting to Christianity or through manumission (the legal process by which an enslaved person could be freed).

In the early years of St. Augustine's existence, enslaved Africans were employed in various tasks—agriculture, domestic service, and labor in the construction of fortifications, such as the Castillo de San Marcos. However, some enslaved Africans managed to gain their freedom, either by escaping or through the legal system. The city became a haven for runaway slaves from English colonies to the north, particularly from the Carolinas, who sought refuge in St. Augustine.

By the late 17th century, St. Augustine had earned a reputation as a sanctuary for runaway enslaved people. Spanish Florida was one of the few places in the Americas where enslaved Africans could find a degree of autonomy. In 1687, the Spanish crown issued the *Decree of Freedom* for enslaved Africans who converted to Catholicism and agreed to defend the Spanish crown. This decree allowed a number of formerly enslaved people to integrate into St. Augustine's society, where they were given land, houses, and other resources.

One of the most significant developments in St. Augustine's African history occurred in 1738 when the Spanish established the *Fort Mose* settlement just north of the city. Fort Mose became the first legally sanctioned free Black settlement in what is now the United States. It was established as a defense against British

162

colonial forces in the Carolinas and became home to a significant number of African refugees who had escaped from British slavery in the southern colonies. The settlers at Fort Mose were not only free but also served as soldiers in the Spanish military, protecting Florida's borders.

In 1763, Spain ceded Florida to Britain in exchange for Havana, Cuba, after the Seven Years' War. Under British rule, the dynamics of Black life in St. Augustine shifted dramatically. The British government implemented policies that were more hostile to free Africans, leading to the dismantling of Fort Mose and the displacement of its inhabitants. Many of the residents fled to Cuba or back to the Spanish-controlled territories.

When Florida was ceded back to Spain in 1783, the African population of St. Augustine faced new challenges but also new opportunities for freedom and prosperity. During the early years of the 19th century, St. Augustine became home to many free Black people, some of whom had come from the northern United States or from other parts of the Caribbean. These free Black residents contributed to the city's economy and society, but they were also caught in the rising tensions leading to the Seminole Wars (1817–1858).

The presence of enslaved people in St. Augustine, as in the rest of Florida, grew in the early 1800s, but Black communities in the city also continued to resist. By the time Florida became a state in 1845, St. Augustine had a significant African-descended population. These

Black residents—both free and enslaved—played an important role in the social fabric of the city, although their lives were fraught with the constant threat of displacement, violence, and the tightening grip of slavery.

During the American Civil War, St. Augustine—along with much of Florida—was a battleground between Union and Confederate forces. The city's African-descended population faced tremendous upheaval during this time. Many enslaved people fled to Union lines, seeking freedom and the protection of the Union Army. St. Augustine, captured by Union forces in 1862, became an important base for African Americans seeking refuge from slavery.

The history of the Black population in St. Augustine is a story of resilience, resistance, and eventual triumph. From the early days of slavery under Spanish rule to the fight for freedom and equality during the Civil Rights Movement, Black Floridians in St. Augustine have always been integral to the city's development and identity.

Nestled just north of St. Augustine, Florida, Fort Mose (also known as *Gracia Real de Santa Teresa de Mose*) holds a unique and powerful place in American history. Established in 1738, it was the first legally sanctioned free Black settlement in what would later become the United States. Its creation marked a revolutionary moment in the history of slavery and freedom, as it provided an unprecedented opportunity for Africans to escape the brutal conditions of enslavement and live in autonomy. Fort Mose was not just a fort; it was a symbol of resistance,

164

resilience, and self-determination—a sanctuary for Africans seeking liberation in a world dominated by colonial oppression.

The roots of Fort Mose lie in the policies of the Spanish Empire in Florida, which differed markedly from the practices in British colonies. From the time of St. Augustine's founding in 1565, Spanish Florida became a haven for enslaved Africans fleeing British-controlled areas. Unlike English settlements, where slaves were treated as property with little hope of gaining freedom, Spanish Florida allowed enslaved people the possibility of freedom through escape, conversion to Catholicism, and service to the Spanish Crown.

By the late 17th century, as word spread of the refuge offered by the Spanish, St. Augustine became a critical destination for Africans seeking freedom. Spanish authorities encouraged runaway slaves from the British colonies to come to Florida, offering them sanctuary. Those who arrived were often granted their freedom if they agreed to serve the Spanish Crown, convert to Catholicism, and pledge loyalty to the Spanish King.

This policy created a significant free Black population in St. Augustine by the early 18th century. Among these free Black men and women were individuals who had escaped from the brutalities of slavery in the British colonies, particularly from the Carolinas and Georgia. With the increasing number of African refugees and freedmen in the region, the Spanish Crown decided to establish a formal settlement for them, one that would serve both as a military outpost and a refuge for the growing population of freed Africans.

The First free Black Settlement in the United States: Fort Mose 1738

In 1738, the Spanish colonial authorities established Fort Mose about two miles north of St. Augustine, along the Matanzas River. The fort was not only a military installation but also a refuge for African people who had escaped slavery and pledged their service to the Spanish Crown. This settlement was founded on the promise of freedom and was designed to defend Spanish Florida from the growing threat of British forces in the southern colonies.

Fort Mose's founding is inextricably tied to the events surrounding the British Empire's expansion into the southern colonies. The British were encroaching on Spanish Florida, and Spanish authorities knew they needed to bolster their defenses. The fort was placed strategically to guard the approach to St. Augustine, and its inhabitants—primarily people of African descent—were trained as soldiers to help defend the Spanish colony from British attacks.

Many of the first inhabitants of Fort Mose were formerly enslaved Africans who had fled from the British colonies of South Carolina and Georgia, where slavery was extremely oppressive. These men, women, and children sought refuge under the protection of the Spanish, where they were granted freedom and land in exchange for their military service.

167

The residents of Fort Mose were not merely soldiers. They were also farmers, builders, and community members who formed the foundation of a new, free Black community. The settlement allowed its residents to establish a sense of autonomy and pride, as they carved out a space where they could live independently from the oppressive systems of slavery in the British colonies. The freedom they found in Fort Mose was a direct challenge to the established racial and colonial hierarchies that existed in the Americas at the time.

While Fort Mose's primary purpose was military defense, it was also a thriving community. The Black settlers, many of whom had been enslaved, created a stable and self-sufficient society. They built homes, cultivated crops, and formed tight-knit bonds. The fort's military garrison, consisting of free Black soldiers, was also essential in defending the Spanish colony from British forces.

The residents of Fort Mose practiced Catholicism, a central aspect of their cultural and social life, as it was a condition for their freedom under Spanish law. Catholic missionaries played an important role in the spiritual lives of the community, and the church became a place of congregation, celebration, and solidarity.

Although life at Fort Mose was not without its hardships, particularly given the constant threat of British military action, the settlement provided its residents with an opportunity to create their own future—one free from the chains of slavery. The people of Fort Mose were not just passive recipients of freedom; they were active participants in shaping the course of their lives and their community. Many took on roles as skilled artisans, farmers, and soldiers, helping to sustain the settlement both economically and militarily.

The soldiers of Fort Mose, who were primarily African men and women, played a key role in the military defense of St. Augustine. Their training and strategic importance meant that they were integral to the protection of the Spanish colony from British invasions. They also provided crucial assistance in maintaining order and stability in the region.

In 1740, Fort Mose's role as a strategic military defense post became its undoing. British forces, led by General James Oglethorpe of the Georgia colony, launched an assault on St. Augustine, hoping to capture the city and disrupt Spanish control of Florida. In June of that year, Oglethorpe's troops attacked Fort Mose. Despite the fort's defenders putting up a fierce resistance, the British forces overwhelmed the settlement, capturing many of its residents.

The fall of Fort Mose was a significant blow to the free Black community. Many of the soldiers and civilians were forced to flee, and some sought refuge in St. Augustine or escaped further into Spanish-controlled territory. Though the fort was destroyed, the legacy of Fort Mose lived on through its people, whose fight for freedom and autonomy left an indelible mark on the history of Florida and the United States.

Although Fort Mose was destroyed in 1740, its legacy endured. It represented the first time in the Americas that formerly enslaved Africans were granted freedom through a formal legal process and allowed to form a thriving, independent community. The settlement's existence challenged the prevailing notion of racial inferiority and demonstrated that Black people, even in the face of colonial oppression, could create their own paths to freedom.

In the centuries that followed, the significance of Fort Mose faded into obscurity, but in the 20th century, it was rediscovered as a symbol of African American resistance and resilience. Archaeological excavations at the site have unearthed artifacts and remnants of the fort, and in 1994, Fort Mose State Park was established to preserve the site and honor its historical importance.

Fort Mose is now recognized as a National Historic Landmark, a testament to the courage and determination of the Africans who fought for their freedom in colonial Florida. Today, the fort serves as an educational and cultural site, teaching visitors about the role that African Americans played in the early history of the United States. The stories of Fort Mose's inhabitants are part of a larger narrative of freedom, resistance, and empowerment that continues to inspire generations of Americans.

Fort Mose was not just a military fort; it was a symbol of what was possible for African people who, despite centuries of oppression and brutality, found ways to resist, survive, and

170

thrive. As the first free Black settlement in America, Fort Mose represents a foundational moment in the history of freedom and Black resistance in the Americas. Its legacy serves as a powerful reminder of the ability of enslaved and oppressed peoples to carve out spaces of autonomy and build communities of strength and self-determination.

The Architect of Black Fraternalism: Prince Hall 1775

Prince Hall (1735–1807) was a visionary and leader whose legacy is deeply woven into the fabric of American history, particularly in the context of Black empowerment, social organization, and fraternalism. Born into slavery in Massachusetts, Hall's life journey epitomized the transition from bondage to freedom, and his work left an indelible mark on the free African American communities of the north. As the founder of the first African American Masonic lodge in America, Hall's contributions extend beyond the realm of Freemasonry and into the fight for racial equality, repatriation, and community cohesion.

Prince Hall was born around 1735 in either West Africa or the West Indies, though his exact birthplace remains uncertain. He was enslaved by William Hall, a prominent Boston merchant, who brought him to Massachusetts. Little is known about Hall's early years under slavery, but by the time of the American Revolution, he had gained his freedom, likely through his master's death or manumission.

Once free, Hall became a member of Boston's Freedmen's community, which, though small, was vibrant and growing. Slavery was still entrenched in the northern states, however Boston served as the center of the abolitionist movement, and it had a growing number of free Black citizens. Hall, like many other free African Americans, had to navigate a society that

172

restricted Black people's access to education, political power, social and economic mobility.

Many recognize Prince Hall's legacy in the creation of Black American Freemasonry, but few consider his support of repatriation to Africa campaigns. The story begins in 1775 when Prince Hall, along with fourteen other free Black men, were initiated into the Masonic fraternity by the Lodge of St. John in Boston, Massachusetts. The Lodge of St. John was an arm of the British military, and Hall's entry into the group was a significant event, offering him access to a network of ideas and principles that would profoundly shape his philosophy on freedom, self-determination, and social cohesion.

Faced with the rejection of white supremacists in Boston, Prince Hall and his colleagues turned to a radical course of action. In 1784, Hall petitioned the Grand Lodge of England for a charter to form an independent African American lodge. The Grand Lodge granted his request, and in that same year, Hall and his brethren established African Lodge No. 1 in Boston.

Prince Hall's creation of African Lodge No. 1 marked the birth of Prince Hall Freemasonry, which became a cornerstone for the organization of African American social and political life in Roxbury, Massachusetts. This lodge would eventually grow into the larger Prince Hall Masonic tradition, with lodges spread throughout the United States, serving as a critical social network for African Americans during a time when they were excluded from most other public spaces and institutions.

At its core, Freemasonry was, and still is, based on a set of ethical and moral teachings that emphasize the values of fraternity, charity, and mutual support. Prince Hall Freemasonry took these ideals and applied them in a context that emphasized racial solidarity and self-determination. Hall's Freemasonry offered African Americans a space for personal and communal upliftment. The lodge became a symbol of Black unity, providing not only social opportunities but also educational resources, mutual aid, and political activism. For many African Americans, particularly in the 18th and 19th centuries, Freemasonry was one of the few spaces where they could build relationships and achieve a sense of equality.

Hall himself was deeply committed to the principles of Masonic fraternity, which included self-discipline, charity, and the pursuit of wisdom. These values were critical to the improvement of African American communities, particularly in a time when systemic racism relegated Black people to the margins of society. Hall's dedication to these principles was a direct challenge to the prevailing racial hierarchies of the time, providing Black people with the tools to resist oppression and uplift themselves socially and economically.

Prince Hall believed in the importance of education and moral development as the key to improving the conditions of Black people. In his speeches and writings, Hall emphasized that true

174

freedom for Black people would come not only through the abolition of slavery but also through the development of strong moral character, financial independence, and the pursuit of knowledge.

Prince Hall's Masonic work was inseparable from his activism in the abolitionist movement. Hall believed that true freedom could only be achieved through the abolition of slavery and the attainment of full civil rights for Black people. His involvement in the abolitionist movement was multifaceted, as he used his position as the leader of African Lodge No. 1 to rally other Black people to the cause of freedom. He was not just a Freemason but also a vocal advocate for the equality and rights of African Americans, both in the legal realm and in the everyday social practices that kept Black people subjugated.

In 1780, Prince Hall petitioned the Massachusetts legislature, requesting that the state abolish slavery. His petition was one of the earliest formal attempts by an African American leader to address the issue of slavery at the state level. The petition was a bold move for a man whose race and social standing left him vulnerable to persecution or death, but it reflected Hall's deep commitment to the cause of liberty and justice.

Though Massachusetts did not immediately respond to Hall's petition, the seeds of abolition began to take root in the state, and by 1783, slavery was effectively abolished in Massachusetts due to a series of court decisions and legislative actions. This victory was in part due to the efforts of Prince Hall and others who fought tirelessly for Black freedom.

Prince Hall's legacy is profound and far-reaching. His creation of African Lodge No. 1 marked a pivotal moment in the history of African American social organizations, and his work as an abolitionist, educator, and political activist laid the groundwork for future generations of Black leaders. Prince Hall Freemasonry provided a framework for solidarity and collective action, which would become an important part of the African American struggle for civil rights in the 19th and 20th centuries.

Prince Hall's significance extends beyond Freemasonry. He was a pioneer in the fight for African American civil rights, a role that would be picked up and carried forward by leaders such as Frederick Douglass, W.E.B. Du Bois, and Martin Luther King Jr. His work laid the foundation for the Black community's fight for equal rights and opportunities in a society that sought to deny them.

In conclusion, Prince Hall's life and legacy are a testament to the power of organization, leadership, and moral vision. From his beginnings as an enslaved person in Massachusetts to his establishment of African American Freemasonry and his advocacy for abolition, Prince Hall left a profound impact on the trajectory of African American freedom. His work provided a model of unity and empowerment that continues to inspire communities to this day.

Free African Union Society of Newport, Newport Gardner 1780

The early 19th century was a time of immense change for African Americans in the United States, particularly for those who had managed to gain their freedom in the northern states. While the southern states were still entrenched in the institution of slavery, free African Americans in cities like Philadelphia, New York, and Boston were laying the foundations for greater social and political autonomy. One of the most significant yet often overlooked examples of this emerging African American self-determination is the Free African Union Society of Newport, Rhode Island, and its prominent member, Newport Gardner. This society not only provided a platform for African American social support but also reflected the aspirations for education, equality, and community solidarity among free Black people in the early 19th century.

The Free African Union Society, founded in 1780 in Newport, Rhode Island, was one of the earliest and most influential Black organizations in the United States. It emerged in a city that, despite its active participation in the transatlantic slave trade, was home to a growing free Black population. Newport, at the time, was a thriving port town, and though slavery had been officially abolished in Rhode Island in 1784, the legacy of slavery remained embedded in the region's social and economic fabric.

177

The Free African Union Society was formed to provide support and mutual aid for the free Black community of Newport, who were often subject to discrimination, poverty, and marginalization. The society's stated goals were to promote the well-being of African Americans, facilitate their social and economic advancement, and provide assistance to the widows and orphans of its members. It was a vital institution that enabled African Americans to care for their own, bypassing the limited or hostile options available within white-dominated society.

The organization was, in many ways, a precursor to the later abolitionist and civil rights organizations that would emerge throughout the 19th and 20th centuries. It was also rooted in the religious and moral imperative of mutual care, and its members were often devout Christians who believed in the importance of solidarity and communal responsibility. It became a place where free African Americans could unite to support one another in the face of persistent racial discrimination.

One of the most notable figures associated with the Free African Union Society was Newport Gardner, a man whose life and contributions would leave an indelible mark on the history of African American resistance and cultural preservation. Newport Gardner was born in 1746, likely in West Africa, and was brought to the United States as a slave. His early years were defined by the brutal realities of slavery, but Gardner's resilience and intellect would eventually lead him to freedom and prominence in Newport.

178

Gardner's story is remarkable not only for his eventual liberation but for his efforts to carve out a space for African American intellectual and cultural development. He was enslaved by a wealthy Newport merchant, who eventually sold him. Gardner's fate seemed sealed until his eventual purchase of his own freedom in 1774, an act that was both an extraordinary personal achievement and a symbolic moment in the broader context of African American autonomy in the late 18th century. Gardner worked as a servant, but he also began to use his spare time to educate himself, eventually mastering English and learning to read and write. His intellectual pursuits, particularly his engagement with Christian theology and philosophy, would influence his later contributions to the African American community.

By the time the Free African Union Society was founded in 1780, Gardner had already established himself as an influential figure within the Newport Black community. His leadership in the society, where he became one of its most respected members, reflected his deep commitment to the cause of Black empowerment, education, and mutual aid. Gardner believed that African Americans should not only be free in the political sense but should also be free in their minds, in their cultures, and in their institutions.

Newport Gardner's work within the Free African Union Society can be understood in the context of his broader philosophy on freedom and equality. For Gardner, the struggle for freedom was not solely about escaping the chains of slavery—it was also about creating opportunities

179

for African Americans to flourish intellectually, socially, and economically. His leadership in the Free African Union Society was instrumental in organizing educational initiatives, as well as efforts to support and care for widows, orphans, and the sick.

Gardner's role in the society was both practical and philosophical. He worked with others to raise funds, organize events, and create educational programs that would enable African Americans in Newport to thrive. Through the society, Gardner helped establish one of the earliest schools for African American children in Newport, ensuring that young people in the community had access to education. In a time when white supremacy was embedded in every aspect of society, from education to employment, providing Black children with the tools for self-determination was a radical act.

Moreover, Gardner's leadership extended beyond the realm of education. He became a central figure in the development of an African American cultural and social identity in Newport. He encouraged African Americans to take pride in their heritage and to support one another economically. The Free African Union Society was a space where individuals could express their shared concerns, organize for mutual benefit, and stand in solidarity in the face of external prejudice.

In addition to his educational initiatives, Gardner was also involved in organizing collective efforts to purchase the freedom of enslaved African Americans. This practice, known as

180

"buying freedom," was one of the ways that free Black people could directly challenge the institution of slavery. It was a process that required great resourcefulness and collective action. Through the Free African Union Society, Gardner worked with others to raise funds and organize efforts that would secure the release of enslaved people in Newport.

Newport Gardner's work with the Free African Union Society represents a crucial chapter in the story of African American self-determination. At a time when African Americans were struggling to build a life in the shadow of slavery, Gardner and the society's members were creating something radically new: a space for Black people to live independently and without reliance on white institutions. Gardner's belief in the power of education and mutual aid was ahead of its time and would become a central tenet of African American political thought in the years that followed.

Gardner's legacy extends beyond the immediate impact of the Free African Union Society. His efforts to create educational opportunities and advocate for the abolition of slavery foreshadowed many of the themes that would emerge in the abolitionist movements of the 19th century. Figures like Frederick Douglass, who would later become one of the most famous abolitionists in American history, would follow in Gardner's footsteps, championing education and self-reliance as central components of the fight for Black freedom.

Though much of Gardner's personal life remains shrouded in history, his influence on the African American community in Newport and beyond cannot be overstated. Through the Free African Union Society, he and his fellow activists were laying the groundwork for the broader Black freedom movements of the 19th century. His belief in the importance of community, education, and self-determination would echo through the lives of generations of African Americans who fought for justice, equality, and freedom.

The Free African Union Society of Newport, Rhode Island, was a pioneering organization that laid the foundation for African American community-building, social activism, and intellectual empowerment. Its most prominent member, Newport Gardner, played a critical role in its development, advocating for education, mutual aid, and the abolition of slavery. His life and work stand as a testament to the enduring power of African American self-determination and the ongoing struggle for racial justice.

Through the Free African Union Society, Gardner not only provided immediate support for African Americans in Newport but also set the stage for the broader social and political movements that would unfold in the centuries to come. His work continues to inspire the ongoing fight for Black autonomy, justice, and equality in America.

Black Loyalist in British North America: Moses Wilkinson 1783

In the turbulent years of the American Revolution, where battles were fought over ideals of liberty and independence, one group of people stood in a unique and often misunderstood position: the Black Loyalists. These were enslaved and free Black men, women, and children who, for various reasons, chose to support the British side during the conflict. Their stories, filled with hardship, loyalty, and resilience, have often been overshadowed by the dominant narrative of the Revolution. Yet their contributions, sacrifices, and struggles were integral to the events that shaped the course of American history.

This chapter seeks to examine the lives of the Black Loyalists, exploring their motivations for siding with the British, the challenges they faced during the Revolution, and their subsequent fate in the post-war world. Their story is one of complex allegiances, personal survival, and the pursuit of freedom, and it offers a rich and often overlooked perspective on the Revolution's legacy.

The American Revolution, which began in 1775, was primarily a struggle between the Thirteen Colonies and Britain. While the conflict was fueled by desires for independence and self-governance, it was also deeply intertwined with the institution of slavery. The colonies, particularly in the South, were heavily reliant on enslaved labor to maintain their agricultural economies. The British, in turn, saw an

183

opportunity to exploit this system for their own strategic advantage.

For many enslaved Black people, the decision to join the British cause was not simply a matter of political allegiance; it was about securing personal freedom. In 1775, Lord Dunmore, the Royal Governor of Virginia, issued a proclamation offering freedom to any enslaved person who escaped to British lines and joined the royal forces. This declaration, known as Lord Dunmore's Proclamation, had a profound impact on enslaved people throughout the colonies.

The proclamation was a direct response to the growing unrest in the colonies and the need for additional forces to suppress the revolutionaries. However, for Black men and women who were living in bondage, it was seen as a rare opportunity for liberation. Thousands of enslaved people, and even free Blacks, fled their masters and made their way to British lines in hopes of securing their freedom.

The British military, recognizing the potential manpower this would provide, welcomed these individuals with open arms. Black soldiers and laborers were recruited into the British army and navy, where they performed various roles, from combatants to laborers, cooks, and servants. Many of these individuals came to be known as Black Loyalists, as they threw their lot in with the British cause, believing that British rule might offer them the liberty they were denied under American colonial slavery.

The Black Loyalists played a significant role in the Revolutionary War, contributing to the British war effort in several important ways. While their military participation was often relegated to non-combat roles, some Black Loyalists did serve as soldiers, fighting in various battles alongside their British counterparts.

In addition to their service in the military, many Black Loyalists were employed in support roles that were critical to the British army's operations. These roles included cooking, building fortifications, and serving as spies. The British valued their contributions, particularly in the Southern colonies, where their knowledge of local terrain and people was invaluable. In fact, the British army often used Black Loyalists to infiltrate rebel lines or to gather intelligence on the movements of American forces.

The Black Loyalists' loyalty to the British cause was not necessarily a political allegiance to British rule, but rather a desperate bid for personal freedom and survival. Many believed that the British would offer them a better future than the rebellious Americans, who sought independence but did so while maintaining slavery in many of their states.

However, the role of Black Loyalists was not just limited to the military or logistical support. They also played an important part in the larger social fabric of British-occupied areas. For example, in the British-controlled city of New York, Black Loyalists formed their own communities, such as the Black Pioneers—a corps of Black soldiers, laborers, and their

185

families who were essential to British operations during the war.

Despite being promised freedom, the reality for Black Loyalists after the war was far from straightforward. Once the war ended in 1783 with the signing of the Treaty of Paris, which recognized American independence, the fate of the Black Loyalists became a matter of great uncertainty.

The end of the Revolutionary War marked the beginning of a new set of challenges for the Black Loyalists. The Treaty of Paris stipulated that the British would return control of American territory to the newly formed United States, but it also included provisions for the protection of Loyalist property and rights. This was interpreted by many as a promise that Black Loyalists would be resettled in British territories.

In reality, the transition was anything but smooth. While the British government had pledged to honor the freedom of the Black Loyalists, the promises made were often not fully realized. Black Loyalists were promised land, provisions, and support for their resettlement, but many were faced with overcrowded conditions, lack of resources, and harsh winters.

The first large-scale migration of Black Loyalists occurred in 1783, when more than 3,000 Black men, women, and children left New York and other loyalist strongholds to settle in Nova Scotia, a British colony in what is now Canada. The journey to Nova Scotia was perilous, with many Black Loyalists traveling on

186

overcrowded ships. The conditions were appalling, and many died from disease or malnutrition during the journey.

Once they arrived in Nova Scotia, the Black Loyalists faced new challenges. They were given land in the colony's wilderness, but the land was often unsuitable for farming, and the climate was harsh. Many Black Loyalists who had hoped for a better life found themselves struggling with poverty and isolation. Tensions between the Black Loyalists and the white settlers in Nova Scotia were high, as many of the latter resented the idea of Black people receiving land and resources from the British government.

Despite these difficulties, some Black Loyalists managed to build stable communities in Nova Scotia. They established settlements such as Birchtown, one of the largest free Black communities in North America at the time, where they built homes, churches, and schools. Over time, some Black Loyalists turned to occupations like shipbuilding, carpentry, and farming to make a living. However, many others found that their hopes for equality and prosperity were never fully realized.

The experience of the Black Loyalists is a complex and often painful chapter in the history of the American Revolution and the history of slavery in the Americas. For these men and women, the American Revolution was not just a war for political independence—it was a war for personal freedom. Their decision to join the British cause was driven by the hope of escaping

187

the brutal conditions of slavery, but the post-war reality was far less promising.

The Black Loyalists left a lasting impact on the communities they established in Nova Scotia and beyond. Many of them later moved to Sierra Leone, where they were part of a resettlement program organized by the British government. These individuals played a significant role in the creation of Freetown, a colony for freed Black people in West Africa, where they established one of the earliest free Black communities in the modern world.

In the centuries since, the story of the Black Loyalists has been largely forgotten or marginalized. Yet their contributions to the American Revolution, their struggles for freedom, and their resilience in the face of adversity are an important part of the larger narrative of the struggle for liberty and equality in North America. The story of the Black Loyalists reminds us that the fight for freedom during the Revolution was not limited to the white colonists who sought independence from Britain, but also included Black men and women who sought freedom from slavery—a goal that, for many, was never fully achieved.

The Black Loyalists were among the most marginalized and forgotten groups of the American Revolution. Their loyalty to the British crown was driven by the hope of escaping enslavement and securing a better life. Yet, despite the promises made to them, their post-war experiences were marked by hardship, displacement, and continued struggle. Their stories, however, are vital to understanding the complexity of the American Revolution and the long and difficult path to freedom for Black people in North America. The Black Loyalists' resilience and courage stand as a testament to their determination to fight for freedom, even in the face of overwhelming odds.

Moses Wilkinson is not a name that many Americans recognize, yet his life story is emblematic of the struggle for freedom and equality that spanned generations. A man of remarkable resilience, Moses was born into slavery, but he would come to be known for his daring efforts to escape bondage and his role in advocating for the rights of the oppressed. His journey from enslavement to freedom reveals not just the painful realities of slavery, but the untold stories of individuals who fought not just for their own liberty, but for the freedom of others.

This chapter seeks to explore the life and legacy of Moses Wilkinson, examining his experiences as a slave, his escape to freedom, and his later role in the abolitionist movement. In doing so, we will gain insight into the broader historical context of slavery and resistance in early America and explore why Moses Wilkinson's story is one that deserves to be remembered.

Moses Wilkinson was born in 1780 in the state of Virginia, at a time when the institution of slavery was deeply entrenched in American society, particularly in the southern states. His exact birth date and details surrounding his early life remain unclear, but it is believed that Moses was born on a large tobacco plantation owned by

189

a wealthy planter named Thomas Wilkinson. As was the case for most enslaved individuals in the South, Moses' early years were defined by forced labor, deprivation, and the complete lack of personal agency.

Growing up on the Wilkinson plantation, Moses was subjected to the harsh conditions that characterized much of the slavery system. He was assigned to work in the fields, alongside other enslaved men and women, cultivating tobacco, cotton, and other crops vital to the plantation's wealth. In addition to grueling physical labor, Moses witnessed the cruelty and violence that plantation owners and overseers often inflicted upon those they enslaved. His own family was torn apart, as was common for enslaved people, and he was separated from his parents at a young age, likely sold off to different plantations.

Though Moses spent much of his youth under the oppressive thumb of slavery, it is clear that from an early age, he developed a strong sense of self and a deep desire for freedom. Little is known about his early education, but some historians believe that Moses was able to learn to read and write, skills that were forbidden to enslaved people in many parts of the South. It is this intellectual and emotional strength, combined with a fierce yearning for autonomy, that would later fuel his escape and his life's work in pursuit of freedom for himself and others.

Moses Wilkinson's path to freedom began in the early 1800s, when the growing abolitionist movement in the North and the increasing tension between the North and South made the institution of slavery a subject of national debate. The idea of escaping slavery was not new, but it was fraught with immense dangers. Slaves who attempted to flee were at risk of being captured and returned to their masters, often suffering brutal punishment for the attempt. Yet, for Moses, the risks of staying were far greater than the risks of fleeing.

In 1810, at the age of 30, Moses decided to take the perilous step of escaping from the Wilkinson plantation. With little more than his wits and determination, he made his way to the North, using the little bit of knowledge he had gathered from other enslaved people and trusted allies about the route to freedom. Whether Moses traveled alone or with the aid of the Underground Railroad is uncertain, as there are no detailed records of his journey. However, it is known that many escaped slaves relied on trusted networks of free blacks, sympathetic whites, and abolitionists who helped guide them on their way.

Moses's journey would have been fraught with hardship and danger. He likely had to travel by night to avoid detection, making his way through dense forests and across rivers, all the while evading slave catchers and the bounty hunters who sought to return escaped slaves to their masters. The Fugitive Slave Act of 1793 had made it even more perilous for escaped slaves, as it allowed any free person to capture and return runaway slaves to the South and offered a reward for their capture.

After weeks of perilous travel, Moses eventually made it to Philadelphia, one of the

191

main hubs of the abolitionist movement. In this city, Moses found safety, support, and a network of individuals who were committed to ending slavery and helping people like him. Philadelphia was a beacon of hope for many enslaved individuals escaping to the North. The city had a growing community of free blacks, abolitionists, and Quakers, all of whom provided essential support to runaway slaves.

Though Moses had succeeded in his escape, his story didn't end there. It was in Philadelphia that Moses's true journey toward activism began.

Upon arriving in Philadelphia, Moses Wilkinson experienced a profound sense of relief, but also a realization that his struggle for freedom was not over. In the North, while slavery was not legal, systemic racism and prejudice still pervaded society. Many freed African Americans lived in poverty, without the same rights or opportunities as white citizens. The path to true equality remained elusive.

Moses, having experienced the harshest of human conditions, was determined to ensure that others could experience the freedom he had won. He soon became involved in the growing abolitionist movement, joining organizations dedicated to the emancipation of enslaved people and the rights of African Americans. He attended abolitionist meetings, contributed to petitions calling for the abolition of slavery, and spoke at public events about his experiences as an enslaved person and his dangerous journey to freedom.

One of Moses's most significant contributions to the abolitionist cause was his work in helping other enslaved people escape. Drawing upon his own experience, Moses became an informal guide and adviser to others attempting to flee the South. Though there are no definitive records of Moses's direct involvement in the Underground Railroad, it is widely believed that he provided guidance and resources to others on their own escapes.

Moses Wilkinson also became an advocate for the integration of African Americans into the broader fabric of Northern society. His efforts were not just about ending slavery in the South but also about securing civil rights for freedmen in the North. He spoke out against the segregation and racial discrimination that continued to impact free Blacks, arguing that liberty could not truly be realized until African Americans were afforded full equality under the law.

The exact details of Moses Wilkinson's later life remain somewhat mysterious. It is believed that he lived in Philadelphia for much of his adult life, where he continued his advocacy for the abolition of slavery and the rights of African Americans. However, unlike many other abolitionists, Moses did not become a widely recognized figure in historical records. His name does not appear frequently in the letters, publications, or histories of the era, which may be a reflection of the larger erasure of Black voices from the mainstream historical narrative.

Nonetheless, Moses's work was part of a broader movement that contributed to the eventual end of slavery in the United States. His advocacy and activism helped to lay the groundwork for the more organized abolitionist efforts that would follow, culminating in the Emancipation Proclamation of 1863 and the Thirteenth Amendment of 1865.

Today, Moses Wilkinson's story remains largely forgotten, but it is essential that we remember him as one of the countless men and women who fought for the freedom of others. His life is a testament to the power of resilience and the belief that, even in the face of unimaginable adversity, one individual can make a profound difference.

Moses Wilkinson's life offers a powerful reminder of the complexity of the fight for freedom in America. Born into slavery, he managed to escape to freedom, and in doing so, not only changed his own life but became an advocate for others seeking the same liberty. His work as an abolitionist, his efforts to guide other enslaved people to freedom, and his commitment to racial equality are a testament to his character and dedication to the cause of justice. Moses Wilkinson may not be a household name, but his legacy lives on in the work of those who continue to fight for freedom, equality, and justice. His story is one that should be remembered as a vital chapter in the long, ongoing struggle for Black liberation.

The African Methodist Episcopal Church Richard Allen 1783

The birth of the African Methodist Episcopal (AME) Church is a story rooted in struggle, faith, and the desire for self-determination. At the center of this pivotal moment in American religious and social history stands Richard Allen, a man whose vision and determination shaped the spiritual lives of African Americans for generations to come. His life and the founding of the AME Church reflect both the painful history of slavery and racial oppression in America and the resilience of the African American community in the pursuit of freedom—both spiritual and worldly.

Richard Allen was born into slavery on February 14, 1760, in Philadelphia, Pennsylvania, to a couple of African descent. His early years were defined by the brutality of slavery, which denied him even the most basic freedoms. However, Allen's story was not one of passive submission to the system of oppression. From an early age, Allen exhibited an innate curiosity about the world around him, especially in matters of faith. As a young man, he was introduced to Christianity and, under the guidance of a Methodist preacher, Allen experienced a profound spiritual awakening. His conversion to Christianity was the beginning of a journey that would radically alter the course of his life.

In his early twenties, Allen became a devout Methodist, a religion that, despite its association

195

with the dominant white society, offered a sense of solace and a platform for spiritual expression. His devotion to the faith was so intense that, despite the hardship of his enslaved status, he began to read scripture and practice his religion diligently. His dedication caught the attention of the Methodist community, and in 1780, at the age of 20, he purchased his freedom for $2,000.

The Methodist Church in the 18th century was known for its emphasis on personal piety, charity, and the salvation of the soul. Its message, particularly its emphasis on personal salvation, resonated with many African Americans, both free and enslaved. Methodism's doctrine allowed for the possibility of an egalitarian spiritual community where black men and women could worship alongside white Christians, even though the practice was often hindered by the prevailing racial attitudes of the time. For many African Americans, the Methodist Church represented an avenue for spiritual freedom, but it also presented a paradox. While the Church preached spiritual equality, it also participated in the racial injustices of the time, as segregation and racial discrimination pervaded many church services.

Allen's involvement in the Methodist Church, though initially marked by a sense of belonging, would eventually expose the deep racial divides within the faith community. One such instance occurred in 1787 at St. George's Methodist Church in Philadelphia, where Allen and a group of fellow African American worshippers were forcibly removed from the church during a prayer service. They had been kneeling in prayer when they were told by white parishioners to vacate their seats because they were not allowed to worship in the same space as the white members. This incident, though painful, served as a galvanizing moment in Allen's life. It highlighted the stark limitations placed upon African Americans within the Methodist Church, even as its teachings offered a promise of spiritual equality.

After being ousted from St. George's, Allen and the other African American worshippers began meeting privately in their homes for prayer and worship. It was during these informal gatherings that the idea of creating a separate congregation for African Americans within the Methodist tradition was born. In 1794, Allen, alongside a small group of African American Methodists, founded the Bethel African Methodist Episcopal Church in Philadelphia. This was a pivotal moment in American religious history. Bethel would become the first independent black church in the United States, marking the beginning of the AME Church.

The creation of the AME Church was not simply a matter of separating from white congregations; it was a statement of self-determination, pride, and autonomy for African Americans. Allen believed that African Americans needed their own religious space to worship freely, without the constraints and indignities imposed by segregation and racism. The AME Church was to be a church by African Americans, for African Americans. It would offer not only spiritual support but also a platform for social activism and a rallying point for black empowerment.

197

In 1799, the church was officially incorporated, and Allen was ordained as a minister. Under his leadership, the AME Church began to grow rapidly, attracting African American members from across the northern states. Allen's vision extended beyond simply establishing a place for worship; he sought to build a robust and sustainable institution that could nurture the intellectual, social, and political lives of African Americans. He believed that the church could play a critical role in the fight for justice, equality, and freedom, particularly as slavery continued to ravage the southern states.

The early years of the AME Church were marked by both external and internal struggles. Externally, Allen and the AME Church faced significant opposition from white Methodists, who viewed the establishment of an independent black denomination as a direct challenge to their authority. In fact, the Methodist Episcopal Church (MEC) sought to prevent Allen and others from establishing an independent church, claiming that the African American Methodist community was part of their jurisdiction. However, Allen and his followers were undeterred. They pursued legal avenues to secure their independence, and in 1816, they formally established the African Methodist Episcopal Church at the first General Conference held in Philadelphia. This conference marked the formalization of the denomination and established the AME Church as the first independent black denomination in the United States.

Internally, the AME Church faced challenges in terms of its governance and organization. As a new denomination, it needed to develop structures for leadership, discipline, and mission. Allen and his fellow leaders worked tirelessly to lay the foundation for a church that could withstand the challenges of the time. The denomination was grounded in a belief in education and empowerment, and its early leaders sought to establish schools, publish literature, and support the broader African American community in their pursuit of freedom.

The legacy of Richard Allen and the African Methodist Episcopal Church is one of resilience, faith, and justice. Allen's commitment to his faith, his people, and his vision for a just society laid the groundwork for what would become one of the most influential religious institutions in the African American community. Over the years, the AME Church would grow exponentially, establishing congregations across the United States and around the world. Its influence would extend beyond the realm of religion, serving as a force for social change during the abolitionist movement, the Civil Rights Movement, and beyond.

Allen's pioneering spirit and dedication to his community made him a key figure in American history. By founding the AME Church, he created a spiritual home for African Americans who had been marginalized and disenfranchised by both society and the church. His legacy endures not only in the continued growth of the AME Church but also in the broader struggle for racial equality and justice. His story reminds us

199

that faith, when combined with a commitment to justice, can be a powerful force for transformation in both the spiritual and worldly realms.

In the years following Allen's death in 1831, the African Methodist Episcopal Church would continue to grow and thrive, becoming a symbol of African American resistance to oppression. The church's roots in Allen's vision of freedom, equality, and social justice would continue to shape the African American experience in the United States for centuries to come.

The African Meeting House of Boston: Primus Hall 1798

Primus Hall (February 29, 1756 – March 22, 1842), son of the esteemed Prince Hall, a renowned abolitionist, soldier in the American Revolutionary War, and founder of Prince Hall Freemasonry, stands as one of the most influential figures in the early fight for Black education and civil rights in America. Born into slavery, Primus Hall's life reflects the arduous journey of an individual who, despite the constraints of his birth, shaped a powerful legacy as a community leader, educator, and abolitionist.

Though he was given the name Primus Trask as a child, after being sold into slavery to a man named Ezra Trask, he became best known as Primus Hall, the son of Prince Hall. While much of his early life was shaped by the brutal realities of enslavement, it was Hall's commitment to education and Black empowerment that would define his life's work and legacy. His efforts helped forge a path for future generations of African Americans to claim their place in American society, particularly in the areas of education, self-determination, and civic involvement.

Primus Hall's birth in 1756 came during a time when slavery was deeply entrenched in both the North and South of America. His mother, an unnamed African woman, was enslaved, and his father, Prince Hall, was a free Black man. At some point in Hall's infancy, he was separated from his

201

family and sold into slavery to Ezra Trask, a merchant in Boston, Massachusetts. This marked the beginning of a life under the brutal system of slavery, but it also set the stage for a profound connection to the fight for freedom, which would dominate Hall's later years.

It was through the efforts of his father, Prince Hall, that Primus Hall eventually found his way to freedom. Prince Hall was a pivotal figure in the African American community in Boston, known for his leadership in abolitionist causes and his role as a founding member of Prince Hall Freemasonry, an organization dedicated to advancing the social, political, and economic welfare of Black Americans. Hall's liberation came at a young age, and he began to grow into the influential figure he would become, shaped by the values of leadership, self-determination, and education instilled by his father.

While little is known about his early years after gaining freedom, Primus Hall's ties to Boston's free Black community and his father's legacy would provide him with a strong foundation on which to build his life and work.

Primus Hall's most enduring legacy is his founding of a school for African American children in 1798, one of the first of its kind in the United States. In an era where Black people were largely excluded from formal education, Hall understood that education was essential to the empowerment and upliftment of African Americans. His vision was rooted in the belief that an educated populace would be better equipped to fight against the institution of slavery and fight for civil rights.

Hall began his educational endeavor by opening a school in his own home, providing instruction to Black children who had limited or no access to education. However, the growing demand for Black education in Boston soon required a more formal space. In 1806, the school moved to the African Meeting House, the first Black church in the United States, located in Boston's Beacon Hill neighborhood. This space not only served as an educational institution but also became a center for the Black community's political, social, and spiritual life.

During the next nearly four decades, Primus Hall continued to raise funds to keep the school running, ensuring that future generations of Black children would have access to an education that promoted literacy, moral development, and a sense of social responsibility. By 1835, Hall had successfully established a thriving institution that provided crucial educational opportunities to African American youth at a time when most schools would not admit Black children.

As the son of Prince Hall, who was known for his role in the abolitionist movement and his work in Prince Hall Freemasonry, Primus Hall was inherently placed in a leadership position within the African American community in Boston. Much like his father, who had fought tirelessly for Black civil rights and for the establishment of Black institutions, Primus Hall was also a vocal advocate for Black education and abolition.

His work as an educator was just one aspect of his broader commitment to advancing the freedom and well-being of Black Americans. As a prominent community leader, Hall was actively involved in the civic life of Boston's Black population, which included organizing, fundraising, and advocating for the interests of free Black people in a city where racial discrimination was still widespread. Despite the growing influence of racist laws and societal constraints, Hall worked alongside other leading Black Bostonians, including his father's fellow Freemasons, to ensure that African Americans had the resources they needed to build independent institutions.

Hall's advocacy was particularly focused on the importance of self-sufficiency within the Black community, and he believed strongly in Black autonomy. He was convinced that the future success of Black Americans depended on their ability to organize independently and to cultivate their own leaders, schools, and economic opportunities.

Primus Hall's efforts in establishing and maintaining a school for African American children were not without challenges. Throughout his years as a teacher and advocate, Hall faced constant struggles in raising the funds needed to support his school. As with many social reformers and educators of his time, Hall had to work tirelessly to persuade both the Black and white communities to contribute to his cause. His determination, however, was unwavering. Hall was dedicated to the idea that Black people could rise above the systemic oppression they faced through education, which he saw as a key weapon in the battle for freedom.

Beyond his work with the school, Hall also served as a symbol of Black intellectual and political leadership. His position within Boston's free Black community made him a trusted voice in abolitionist circles, where he advocated for the immediate abolition of slavery and the integration of African Americans into public life.

Hall's involvement in the African Meeting House was also significant, as it not only functioned as a place of worship but also as a site of political and social gatherings for the Black community. Hall played a role in bringing together various factions of the Black community to work toward common goals, including the establishment of Black schools, anti-slavery activism, and the fight for civil rights.

Primus Hall passed away on March 22, 1842, but his legacy as a pioneer of Black education and community leadership lived on long after his death. His contributions to the cause of Black education in America, particularly his work in Boston, would pave the way for future generations of Black scholars and activists. The African Meeting House, where his school operated, would go on to be an important symbol of the resilience and determination of the African American community.

Though much of the history surrounding Primus Hall's life has been overshadowed by other figures of the era, his work as an educator, activist, and leader in the struggle for Black liberation stands as a testament to the power of education in shaping the future of Black Americans. His commitment to teaching, community-building, and abolitionism helped lay the groundwork for the broader civil rights movements of the 19th and 20th centuries. As a leader, he proved that even in the face of tremendous adversity, the pursuit of knowledge and equality could serve as a powerful means of resistance.

In Boston, where his name has been somewhat forgotten in popular history, Primus Hall's life continues to stand as an example of the transformative power of education, the need for Black self-determination, and the relentless pursuit of freedom and equality for all.

Response to the American Colonization Society: James Forten 1817

James Forten was born on September 2, 1766, in Philadelphia, Pennsylvania, into a time of turbulence and transformation in American history. The child of free African American parents, Forten's life would come to embody the promise of self-determination and freedom, as well as the struggles that came with achieving these ideals in a nation that was still grappling with its own contradictions around race and liberty.

Forten was born into a world where freedom was anything but guaranteed for Black people. His father, Thomas Forten, was a free man of African descent who worked as a tailor, but his mother, a woman of mixed African and European heritage, played a more influential role in his upbringing. Though his parents were free, the young James Forten lived in a city that was marked by stark divisions between the enslaved and free Black communities, as well as a stark contrast between rich and poor.

At the age of eight, James's life took a tragic turn. His father passed away, leaving his family in precarious financial circumstances. To help support his family, James became an apprentice to a sailmaker—a decision that would alter the trajectory of his life. In this early job, James learned a trade that would eventually become the key to his financial success and personal freedom.

The sailmaking business was a booming industry in Philadelphia at the time, and it offered James an opportunity to rise above the limitations placed upon him due to his race. However, opportunities were few for free Black people in the late 18th century, and there was still considerable pressure from both the enslaved and free Black communities to prove their worth.

In 1781, during the closing years of the American Revolution, Forten's life took another unexpected turn. At the age of 15, he enlisted in the Continental Navy. Although free Black men were generally barred from service in the military at the time, Forten joined the crew of the *Royal Louis*, a privateer ship that was engaged in naval combat against the British.

Forten's time in the navy exposed him to the complexities of war and the reality of racial discrimination. Though he was treated poorly in some instances because of his race, he distinguished himself by his courage and quick thinking during the battles. When the *Royal Louis* was captured by the British in 1781, Forten was taken prisoner. He was held captive for several months in a British prison before finally being released in a prisoner exchange. The harsh conditions of imprisonment only deepened his resolve to fight for his people's freedom—an ideal that would guide him throughout his life.

The experience of war had a lasting impact on Forten. Not only did it expose him to the struggles of those who fought for liberty, but it also brought into sharp focus the question of freedom for Black people. How could a nation that

208

prided itself on liberty and democracy continue to hold millions in slavery? This question became central to his life's mission.

Upon returning to Philadelphia after his release, Forten reentered the world of sailmaking, where he became a skilled craftsman. Through his apprenticeship, he had gained valuable skills, and now he was able to put those skills to work for himself. Over the years, he managed to save enough money to buy his own sailmaking business. By the 1790s, Forten had established himself as one of the wealthiest and most respected African Americans in Philadelphia.

His business was not just financially successful; it was a place of empowerment. Forten was able to employ other free Black men, giving them opportunities to work and build their own financial independence. He believed strongly in the value of economic self-sufficiency for Black people, and his efforts in business were part of a broader vision to demonstrate that African Americans could thrive and contribute to society on their own terms.

By the early 19th century, Forten was no longer just a successful businessman; he had also become a prominent figure in the African American community. He used his wealth and influence to support causes that advanced the rights of Black people. He was particularly passionate about the abolition of slavery and the improvement of education for Black children, advocating for their right to learn in integrated schools. His work on behalf of education was groundbreaking—he believed that the only way to

209

achieve true equality was through access to knowledge.

Forten's deep sense of justice led him to become a strong advocate for the abolition of slavery. As the nation struggled with the moral contradictions of slavery, Forten used his growing wealth and influence to challenge the institution. He became involved with the Pennsylvania Abolition Society and worked alongside figures like Benjamin Rush, Richard Allen, and Robert Purvis in the fight to end slavery in Pennsylvania and beyond.

But Forten's activism extended far beyond Pennsylvania. He was a member of the American Anti-Slavery Society, which sought to end slavery in the southern states, and he was a vocal critic of the colonization movement, which sought to send free Black people back to Africa. Forten opposed the idea, believing that Black Americans had as much right to live in the United States as any white person.

In his opposition to colonization, Forten argued that African Americans were integral to the fabric of American society. He spoke passionately about the contributions Black people had made to the nation—whether through labor, culture, or military service—and about the injustices they had faced. He saw colonization as a tactic designed to reinforce the social order of white supremacy rather than a genuine solution to the problem of racial inequality.

Forten's activism also included supporting the Underground Railroad, helping to finance the

210

escape of enslaved people to freedom. He became a critical supporter of Black newspapers like Freedom's Journal and The North Star, providing financial contributions and offering guidance on how to spread abolitionist messages. He understood that the fight for freedom could not be won through politics alone; it required changing public opinion and mobilizing people across racial and class lines.

James Forten passed away on March 4, 1842, at the age of 75, but his legacy lives on. He is remembered as a self-made businessman, an advocate for abolition, and a pioneering figure in the fight for racial equality. His life's work showed that African Americans, even in the most difficult circumstances, could thrive and shape the course of history.

Forten's influence extended beyond his lifetime. His family continued his work, with his children becoming active in the abolitionist movement and other social causes. His granddaughter, Charlotte Forten Grimké, became an important educator and writer, and his legacy helped inspire future generations of African Americans to fight for civil rights and social justice.

In a nation that still struggles with issues of race and inequality, James Forten's life serves as a testament to the power of determination, resilience, and an unwavering belief in the cause of freedom. His story reminds us that the fight for equality is not only a political struggle, but a moral and economic one—a struggle for self-determination and the right to shape one's own destiny.

Forten's work transcended his time, offering valuable lessons about economic empowerment, activism, and the importance of fighting for a just society. His story is one of triumph, not just over adversity, but over the forces of oppression that sought to define him by his race rather than his abilities, character, and contributions.

Intellectual Property & Abolition: Thomas L. Jennings. 1821

Thomas L. Jennings (1791–1859) stands as a remarkable figure in both the history of American abolitionism and the early development of patent law in the United States. Born in New York City to free Black parents, Jennings made significant contributions to both social reform and scientific innovation. In a time when Black Americans faced enormous societal challenges, Jennings' life and achievements became a symbol of resilience and agency. His story intertwines the struggles for freedom, intellectual property, and the pursuit of equality, marking him as a pioneer in both the fight for emancipation and the business world.

Thomas Jennings was born to a free African American family in 1791. His parents, as free people of color, provided him with a rare opportunity to receive an education in a society that generally denied it to Black individuals. Jennings' early exposure to both education and the challenges faced by free and enslaved Black people would shape his future endeavors. By the time he reached adulthood, Jennings had established himself as a skilled tradesman, working as a tailor, a profession that provided him with the means to support his family and advocate for freedom.

Jennings was deeply involved in the abolitionist movement, particularly in New York City, where he lived for much of his life. In 1827, New York passed a gradual emancipation law that

213

set a course for ending slavery in the state. However, it was not immediate, and many people remained enslaved, including several in New York City. Jennings became a leader in local abolitionist circles, participating in both public protests and private efforts to aid enslaved people.

Jennings' activism was personal as well as political. In 1830, he was instrumental in securing the freedom of his wife, Elizabeth, who had been born into slavery. Through legal channels, Jennings was able to purchase his wife's freedom, an act that demonstrated his commitment to the abolitionist cause. This personal investment in the liberation of loved ones mirrored the broader abolitionist desire to end slavery once and for all in the United States.

Though Jennings is best known today for his involvement in abolition, it was his invention and subsequent patent that established his historical legacy in the realm of innovation. In 1821, Jennings developed a new method for cleaning and refreshing clothes, which he called "dry scouring." At the time, laundry was a labor-intensive and time-consuming process, especially in urban areas where water was scarce or difficult to access. Jennings' process was a significant improvement over existing methods, which involved washing clothes with water or using harsh chemicals.

Jennings' innovation was based on a chemical process that involved using solvents and a carefully developed set of techniques for removing dirt and stains. By applying his dry-

214

scouring method, clothing could be cleaned more efficiently, and without the damaging effects of water-based cleaning. His technique was revolutionary because it allowed clothes to be freshened and cleaned without the traditional risks of water damage, and it became a highly sought-after service in a rapidly industrializing world.

In 1821, Thomas L. Jennings became the first African American to receive a U.S. patent, a groundbreaking achievement for both him personally and for Black Americans in general. The patent, granted under the title "A Method of Cleaning and Scouring Clothes," marked an important moment in patent law. Jennings' success in securing the patent demonstrated not only his technical skill and ingenuity but also his ability to navigate the legal and bureaucratic systems of the time.

The patent he received was highly significant because it was not just a personal triumph, but it also became a symbol of the potential for Black Americans to contribute to American society beyond the traditional roles imposed on them. Jennings' ability to leverage his intellectual property was a form of economic empowerment and a statement of his worth as an innovator, at a time when Black people were often relegated to subservient and manual labor roles.

Jennings' business, which relied on his patented dry-scouring process, became quite successful. He was able to use his earnings to support his abolitionist activities, including donating money to causes that worked to promote

215

the freedom of enslaved people. His success as an inventor and businessman also provided him with the means to advocate for legal and social reforms for Black Americans. The financial independence he gained through his patent enabled him to take on a more active role in pushing for social justice and equality.

Jennings' work as an inventor was intrinsically tied to his abolitionist efforts. His patent allowed him the means to support his activism, but it also connected his intellectual and entrepreneurial success to the broader struggle for the emancipation of enslaved people. In a time when the opportunities for Black Americans were limited, his patent exemplified the untapped potential of the African American community.

Jennings' success also pointed to a broader contradiction in American society. While Black Americans were being denied basic civil rights, such as the right to vote and the right to own property, they were also capable of extraordinary achievements. Jennings' patent was not just an invention—it was a declaration that Black individuals had the potential for intellectual and economic contributions that were equal to those of any other race.

Jennings' patents also highlighted the significance of intellectual property in the fight for freedom. For African Americans, owning intellectual property provided a form of autonomy that could not easily be taken away. Unlike physical property, intellectual property—such as a patent—represented the ownership of ideas and

216

innovations, creating a potential avenue for Black people to assert their freedom in a society that sought to limit their rights.

Jennings used his financial success and his prominent position in society to further the cause of abolition. He was a member of the New York Anti-Slavery Society and worked alongside other abolitionists, such as Frederick Douglass and Harriet Tubman, to fight for the end of slavery. His wealth allowed him to support the Underground Railroad, provide financial assistance to formerly enslaved people, and fund the activities of other abolitionists.

Thomas L. Jennings' life and achievements were groundbreaking in several respects. As an inventor, he laid the foundation for modern dry-cleaning techniques. As an abolitionist, he demonstrated the power of personal and collective action to fight for freedom and equality. Jennings was not only a trailblazer in his own right but also an inspiration for future generations of African American innovators, activists, and entrepreneurs.

Jennings' patent and his activism symbolize the ways in which Black Americans could use their creativity and skills to challenge the systems of oppression that sought to limit their opportunities. His story stands as a testament to the power of invention, perseverance, and commitment to justice. By securing his patent, Jennings not only improved the daily lives of many Americans, but he also carved a spacc for African Americans in the intellectual and entrepreneurial landscape of the country.

Despite the immense challenges of his time, Jennings was able to use his talents and resources to change the lives of others. His success provided a blueprint for how innovation, abolitionism, and the fight for equality could be intertwined, showing that even in a society built on racial inequality, Black people could rise, create, and transform the world around them.

Thomas L. Jennings' legacy is both an inspiring story of individual achievement and a powerful reminder of the broader struggle for racial justice in America. His patent and his role in the abolitionist movement demonstrate the complex and multifaceted nature of the fight for freedom. Through his innovation, Jennings not only altered the course of American industry but also contributed significantly to the abolitionist movement. His story is one of resilience, creativity, and determination, serving as a reminder that the pursuit of justice and equality requires both intellectual and practical contributions—often from unexpected sources.

First Black to Win a Case Against a White in Court: Sojourner Truth 1828

Sojourner Truth (1797–1883) was one of the most iconic and compelling voices in the abolitionist and women's rights movements. Born Isabella Baumfree in the late 18th century in Ulster County, New York, she would go on to challenge the very foundations of racial and gendered oppression in America. Truth's story is not just that of an escaped slave but of a woman who, against all odds, became a symbol of resilience, liberation, and social change. Her life and legacy continue to inspire generations of activists and ordinary people alike, offering a powerful example of how one voice can challenge and change the course of history.

Sojourner Truth's story begins in enslavement, when she was born as Isabella Baumfree around 1797 in the state of New York. She was born into slavery on the estate of a Dutch-speaking slave owner, Colonel Johannes Hardenbergh, and lived the early years of her life in bondage. Isabella was one of at least 10 children, and like many enslaved people, she grew up knowing nothing but servitude and hardship. The trauma of slavery shaped much of her early existence, but it also sowed the seeds of the strength and resolve she would later display.

As a child, Truth experienced the brutalities of American chattel slavery firsthand. Her early years were marked by physical and emotional abuse, and she was separated from her

219

family members as they were sold off to different slavers. Despite these hardships, Isabella was known for her intelligence, resilience, and work ethic. Though she was illiterate, she retained a sharp memory and deep spiritual beliefs that would later inform her activism.

In 1817, when she was about 20 years old, Isabella's life took a major turn. Her owner, Colonel Hardenbergh's heirs, sold her to another man, John Neely, who forced her to work for years in extremely harsh conditions. In 1826, she successfully sued for her freedom, becoming one of the first Black women to win a court case against a white man in New York State.

Although she was freed from slavery in 1827, the years of her bondage left deep scars on Isabella. Rather than wallow in bitterness, she found solace in her faith. She became deeply religious and was involved in the religious revivalist movement that swept through the United States in the early 19th century. In the early 1830s, she joined a Methodist congregation and became known for her passionate religious sermons.

In 1843, in a powerful act of spiritual transformation, Isabella Baumfree changed her name to Sojourner Truth. This name symbolized her newfound purpose: to travel the country, "sojourning" or journeying from town to town, to spread a message of freedom, equality, and justice to the ears of those who would listen. Her spiritual awakening was matched by a deep sense of personal mission; she saw herself as an instrument of God, chosen to speak out for the oppressed and the disenfranchised.

Her name change was also symbolic of her rejection of the system that had sought to keep her in chains, both literally and metaphorically. Sojourner Truth's public declaration was a testament to her determination to break free not only from physical slavery but from the societal and cultural constraints placed on Black people— particularly Black women.

As an advocate for abolition, Truth was a fierce opponent of slavery. She spoke out against the horrors of enslavement, sharing her own experiences as a former slave and calling for the emancipation of all enslaved people. Her compelling speeches often mixed personal narratives with strong moral and political arguments. Truth's experiences as a mother, former slave, and newly freed Black woman informed her activism, making her one of the most effective and powerful speakers in the abolitionist movement.

She was not just a speaker at abolitionist rallies; she became an active participant in organizing anti-slavery events and in pushing for change. She was known for her confrontational style, confronting both white abolitionists and Southern slaveholders, demanding that they recognize the humanity and rights of Black people. Her impassioned speeches were imbued with her unique perspective as a Black woman, emphasizing that the fight for freedom was inseparable from the fight for gender equality, arguably becoming one of the first philosophers on the intersections of race and gender.

One of Truth's most famous moments as an abolitionist came at the 1851 Women's Rights Convention in Akron, Ohio, where she delivered her iconic "Ain't I a Woman?" speech. The speech was a powerful rebuke to the prevailing notions of race and gender, which often marginalized Black women. In it, she famously challenged the audience's assumptions about what women could do and what rights they were entitled to. Her words, "Ain't I a woman?" resonated as a challenge to both the patriarchy and racism, urging the country to reckon with the intersectionality of race and gender.

In this speech, Truth highlighted her own experience as a mother, as a former slave, and as a woman, all while underscoring the unequal treatment that she and other Black women faced. She confronted the audience with her lived reality, demanding recognition not only as a woman but also as a person with the same rights as any other citizen.

While Truth's abolitionist work was crucial, she also became a staunch advocate for women's rights. Her belief in women's equality was foundational to her activism, and she worked tirelessly to highlight the intersection of race and gender in American society. She often spoke at women's rights conventions and joined forces with other pioneering feminists, like Elizabeth Cady Stanton and Susan B. Anthony, though her relationship with these women was complicated by racial differences and tensions within the movement.

Truth was particularly vocal about the exclusion of Black women from the mainstream women's suffrage movement. She demanded that Black women have the same opportunities to participate in the fight for gender equality and called out the racism that often-sidelined Black women's concerns. Her role in the women's suffrage movement, however, would be largely overshadowed by the white-dominated feminist organizations, which sometimes downplayed the issues of race and class.

Neverless, Sojourner Truth's contribution to Black women's rights cannot be understated. Her advocacy for women's rights went beyond the ballot box and legal equality; she challenged the cultural and societal expectations placed on women, particularly women of color. In Truth's view, equality was not merely about the right to vote or own property—it was about dismantling the entire system of oppression that devalued Black lives, Black bodies, and Black voices.

In her later years, Sojourner Truth continued to speak out, though her health began to decline. She was involved in several important causes, including advocating for the rights of freedmen after the Civil War, supporting the colonization movement (albeit in a modified form), and helping to promote land grants for freed African Americans.

Truth also spent time advocating for the passage of the 13th and 14th Amendments to the

223

Constitution, which granted freedom to slaves
and citizenship to Black Americans. She became
a national figure in the battle for human rights
and left an indelible mark on both the abolitionist
and women's suffrage movements.

Sojourner Truth passed away in 1883 at
the age of 86, but her legacy lived on. She was
remembered as one of the most eloquent and
radical voices of the 19th century, a woman
whose life's work bridged the movements for the
abolition of slavery and women's rights, and
whose fight for justice and equality remains
relevant to this day.

Sojourner Truth's life was a testament to
the power of resistance, resilience, and
transformation. As an abolitionist, a feminist, and
a human rights activist, she stood at the
intersection of multiple struggles, fighting for the
liberation of Black people, for the empowerment
of women, and for the recognition of Black women
as equal participants in the fight for freedom and
dignity. Today, she is celebrated not only for her
pivotal role in these movements but also as a
symbol of the enduring power of one person's
voice to reshape society.

Appeal to the Colored Citizens of the World: David Walker 1829

David Walker (September 28, 1796 – August 6, 1830) was one of the most important, though often overlooked, figures in the abolitionist movement in the early 19th century. His fierce advocacy for the immediate emancipation of enslaved people and his unapologetic calls for Black resistance to slavery and oppression made him both a pioneer of radical abolitionism and a symbol of Black pride and self-determination. Walker's life and legacy embody the passionate defiance of a people who had been denied their basic humanity for centuries but who were determined to fight for their freedom, dignity, and equality.

Born in Wilmington, North Carolina, David Walker's early life was shaped by the institution of slavery. His father was an enslaved man who had gained his freedom, while his mother was free, making Walker legally free from birth. Despite being born free, Walker would come to understand the oppressive and dehumanizing effects of slavery throughout his life. His radical beliefs about freedom, equality, and the immediate abolition of slavery would put him at odds with many of his contemporaries, but also earn him admiration and reverence from those who shared his vision of an emancipated future.

David Walker was born to a free mother and an enslaved father in Wilmington, a port town in North Carolina. His father had gained his freedom from slavery, which meant that Walker himself

225

was born a free man. Despite his free status, Walker witnessed firsthand the horrors of slavery, both in his own family and in the communities around him.

Walker's father had worked on a nearby plantation but, after his emancipation, moved to Charleston, South Carolina. His decision to leave Wilmington was likely motivated by the oppressive and racist climate of the South, where the legal status of Black people—whether free or enslaved—was consistently under threat.

As a young man, Walker moved to Boston, where he became involved with the Black community and was exposed to the intellectual and political currents of the abolitionist movement. At this time, Boston was a hotbed of abolitionism, with prominent figures like Frederick Douglass, William Lloyd Garrison, and Maria Stewart leading the charge for the rights of enslaved and free Black people. Walker's presence in this environment, with its emphasis on civil rights and Black empowerment, likely contributed to his radicalization and the development of his own abolitionist ideology.

While in Boston, Walker worked as a second-hand clothing dealer. His business dealings brought him into contact with a broad cross-section of society, including a variety of Black intellectuals and abolitionist activists. It was here that Walker began to formulate his vision for the liberation of Black people—not just from slavery, but from the oppressive systems of racism and inequality that were deeply ingrained in American society.

David Walker is perhaps best known for his 1830 publication, *David Walker's Appeal to the Coloured Citizens of the World*. This pamphlet, which was distributed widely, called for immediate abolition of slavery and was a direct challenge to the existing racial hierarchies in America. It was written in a tone of defiance, calling upon Black people to resist slavery along with social and economic systems that perpetuated it.

Walker's Appeal was revolutionary in its tone and message. Unlike many other abolitionist leaders who called for gradual emancipation or peaceful change, Walker argued that immediate action was necessary to bring about true freedom for Black people. His message was bold, unapologetic, and uncompromising. He believed that the only way to end slavery was through revolt and armed resistance if necessary. Walker called on enslaved people to rise up and overthrow their oppressors, writing that "the time has come for the Black man to rise, throw off the chains of oppression, and claim the rights he has been denied."

His call for Black resistance was seen as incredibly radical. It rejected the notion that Black people should patiently wait for their freedom to be granted by benevolent slaveholders or the government. Instead, Walker emphasized that the enslaved had a right to fight for their freedom, by any means necessary. In doing so, Walker's appeal became an influential piece of literature that inspired both Black and white abolitionists to take more aggressive stances toward the fight against slavery.

227

Walker's vision was also deeply rooted in Christianity, and he framed his argument for abolition in religious terms. He was deeply critical of the ways in which slaveholders and white Christians used the Bible to justify the system of slavery. For Walker, Christianity demanded the equality of all people, and it was the duty of all Christians—particularly those who identified as followers of Christ—to resist the evils of slavery. His religious argument added a layer of moral authority to his stance and appealed to the growing religious abolitionist movements in both the North and South.

Walker's call for revolt and his radical ideas about Black rights created a firestorm of controversy. His work was seen as dangerous and subversive by both white supremacists and even moderate abolitionists. The pamphlet was banned in the South, and copies of it were burned, while Walker himself was heavily criticized by those who advocated for a more gradual, nonviolent approach to ending slavery.

Walker's radical approach to abolition had significant consequences, both for the movement and for his own life. His pamphlet inspired slave uprisings and was said to have been a major influence on the Nat Turner Rebellion in 1831, an armed insurrection led by an enslaved preacher that resulted in the deaths of dozens of white slaveowners in Virginia. Although Walker himself did not take part in the rebellion, it is clear that his Appeal played a role in galvanizing enslaved people to take direct action against their oppressors.

228

The impact of Walker's Appeal was not confined to enslaved communities. It also energized free Black abolitionists in the North, who took up his call for more radical forms of resistance. His uncompromising stance on the issue of slavery made him a hero for those who believed that nonviolent resistance alone would not be sufficient to dismantle the institution of slavery.

At the same time, Walker's radicalism made him a controversial figure within the broader abolitionist movement. While many abolitionists like William Lloyd Garrison and Frederick Douglass agreed with Walker's core belief that slavery must be abolished immediately, some were uneasy with his call for violent resistance. They worried that his message would alienate potential allies and provoke even more violent repression from slaveholders and the government.

Despite the controversy surrounding his methods, David Walker's legacy as an abolitionist is undeniable. His *Appeal* was a bold declaration of Black empowerment, and it helped shift the abolitionist movement from a more moderate, reformist stance to one that included a demand for immediate action. His advocacy for armed resistance and Black self-determination resonated with future generations of activists, including those in the Civil Rights Movement of the 20th century.

David Walker died in 1830 at the age of 33 under mysterious circumstances, with some speculating that he was poisoned due to his

229

controversial views and activism. His death occurred just one year before the Nat Turner Rebellion, which some historians believe was inspired in part by Walker's *Appeal*. Though he did not live to see the full impact of his work, Walker's ideas continued to resonate in abolitionist circles and beyond, becoming a touchstone for radical resistance movements in the years that followed.

Today, David Walker is remembered as one of the most radical and uncompromising figures in the abolitionist movement. His Appeal remains a foundational text in the history of Black liberation and a testament to the power of direct action in the struggle for freedom and equality. Walker's legacy endures as a reminder that the fight for freedom cannot always be achieved through compromise and gradual change, but sometimes requires bold, revolutionary action to dismantle systems of oppression and create a more just and equal society.

David Walker's radical vision of freedom— one that embraced self-defense, armed resistance, and immediate abolition—was groundbreaking for its time. He was not just an abolitionist but a revolutionary, advocating for total freedom for Black people and a complete overhaul of the systems of racial oppression that had shaped American society for centuries. His work, particularly *David Walker's Appeal*, remains one of the most impassioned calls for freedom in American history, serving as a reminder of the power of Black resistance and self-determination in the face of overwhelming injustice.

Through his fearless advocacy for Black empowerment and immediate emancipation, David Walker helped to expand the scope of the abolitionist movement, challenging both the institution of slavery and the racist attitudes that underpinned American society. His legacy lives on as a symbol of the unrelenting fight for justice, equality, and freedom.

The Origins of Black Separatism: Reverend Lewis "Augustine" Woodson 1831

The early 19th century was a time of profound upheaval in the United States, especially for African Americans. While enslaved people labored in the fields of the South, free African Americans in the North were grappling with systemic racism, limited rights, and an ever-growing sense of racial injustice. Amidst this environment, figures like Richard Allen laid the foundations of religious independence, creating space for black spiritual leadership and social autonomy. In the years that followed, however, the demand for a broader and more radical break from white-dominated institutions grew. One of the lesser-known yet profoundly impactful figures in this movement was Reverend Lewis "Augustine" Woodson, a man whose life and ministry would contribute significantly to the burgeoning idea of black separatism in religion and society.

Lewis Woodson was born in 1791 in the slave state of Virginia, in a world where freedom and opportunity were often denied to African Americans. Raised during a time when slavery was entrenched in the South, Woodson's early experiences with racial discrimination shaped his worldview. Like many African Americans of his time, his early life was marked by hardship, as he lived in the oppressive reality of a society that reduced people of African descent to mere property.

232

Woodson was fortunate, however, in that he was able to experience a significant spiritual awakening early in his life. The Methodist Church, particularly in the Northern states, played a crucial role in shaping the religious consciousness of many free African Americans. Similar to figures like Richard Allen, Woodson found solace and empowerment in Christianity, specifically the Methodist faith. His embrace of the religion was not merely a personal spiritual transformation but also a political one. Christianity provided African Americans a framework to assert their humanity, even as they faced daily racial oppression.

After gaining his freedom, Woodson became deeply involved in religious and social circles within the African American community, both in Virginia and later in Pennsylvania. He worked as a lay preacher and quickly earned a reputation for his eloquence and fervor. His experiences with the Methodist Church, however, were increasingly colored by a sense of betrayal, a feeling that would drive him toward a more radical form of black separatism.

The broader historical and social context of the early 19th century shaped Woodson's thoughts on religion and the need for a distinct black church. In the wake of the American Revolution, many African Americans had come to see the Methodist Church as a potential vehicle for spiritual and social change. For a brief period, the Methodist movement had supported the idea of religious equality, with churches like the Bethel AME Church founded by Richard Allen providing spiritual support to African Americans outside the confines of white-dominated religious institutions.

However, by the 1820s and 1830s, these hopes began to sour as African Americans in the North faced racial discrimination even within the churches they had come to see as places of refuge. In cities like Philadelphia, New York, and Baltimore, black Methodists continued to face segregation within church services. The 1830s, in particular, saw an increase in racial violence, the suppression of black civil rights, and the growing militancy of pro-slavery factions in the South, all of which underscored the enduring gulf between white and black religious life.

Woodson's growing disillusionment with the white-dominated church mirrored the larger rise of black separatism. As African Americans increasingly demanded rights to land, education, and self-governance, religious autonomy became a key part of this push for full liberation. Woodson, witnessing the limitations of the existing black churches in their efforts to challenge white supremacy, began to envision a church that was not simply separate but one that was purposefully autonomous, self-sustaining, and wholly controlled by African Americans.

By 1831, Woodson had become a leading voice in advocating for a truly autonomous black church. This was a pivotal year not only for Woodson but for the entire African American religious experience. In the same year, Nat Turner's rebellion rocked the South, while abolitionist movements were gaining ground in the North. As the country spiraled toward the

234

Civil War, the religious landscape for African
Americans was also changing dramatically.

In this context, Woodson began advocating
for the establishment of a distinct African
American church that would be completely
separate from white Christian institutions. This
was not just a call for a physical separation in
church seating or a division of congregational
spaces, but a theological, institutional, and
cultural break. Woodson's arguments for black
separatism were deeply rooted in a vision of
African American empowerment—spiritually,
socially, and politically.

Woodson argued that African Americans
could no longer afford to exist in a church that
did not see their full humanity. His critique of
white churches focused on their hypocrisy: while
they preached the gospel of equality and
brotherhood, they simultaneously upheld racial
segregation and, in some cases, slavery.
According to Woodson, black people could only
achieve true spiritual freedom by creating their
own religious institutions—churches led by black
clergy, sustained by black congregations, and
shaped by black religious traditions and
experiences.

Woodson's ideas aligned with the broader
black separatist movement that was gaining
traction in the 1830s. Figures like David Walker,
with his incendiary *Appeal to the Colored Citizens
of the World* (1829), and leaders in the black
abolitionist movement were also calling for a
radical rethinking of African American identity
and autonomy. Woodson's religious separatism

235

became an extension of these comprehensive demands for social and political independence.

Woodson's vision for an autonomous black church was closely linked to his belief in the power of education. He argued that black churches should not only serve as places of worship but also as centers for education and social reform. These churches would train black ministers, build schools, and create institutions that could serve as pillars for the African American community. They would provide a counterbalance to the white institutions that were actively working to suppress black advancement.

At the core of Woodson's vision was the belief that African Americans could not rely on white society to provide for their spiritual and intellectual needs. As an educated man himself, Woodson understood that true empowerment would come from self-reliance, especially in the realm of education. Black churches under his leadership would be places where African Americans could receive an education, learn to read and write, and gain the intellectual tools necessary to challenge both slavery and racial inequality.

While Reverend Lewis "Augustine" Woodson did not live to see the full fruition of his dream for a separate black church, his ideas were instrumental in the formation of a more radical form of black religious separatism. His calls for independence, autonomy, and self-determination deeply influenced the growing momentum toward the establishment of independent black churches. Woodson's ideas laid the groundwork for future generations of African American religious leaders who would continue to advocate for the autonomy of black spiritual life.

In the years following Woodson's advocacy, the African American church would emerge as a central institution in the fight for civil rights and social justice. Churches like the AME Church, which had already been established by Richard Allen, continued to thrive, and new denominations like the Christian Methodist Episcopal Church would emerge, expanding the reach of African American religious and social power.

Woodson's vision also set the stage for future African American leaders in both the religious and political arenas, including figures such as Frederick Douglass, who would continue the work of challenging religious and social oppression. In many ways, Woodson's call for religious independence reflected the growing sense of black nationalism that would characterize African American movements throughout the 19th and 20th centuries.

Reverend Lewis "Augustine" Woodson's legacy is one that reflects the deep and abiding relationship between religion and the struggle for racial justice. His advocacy for black separatism in religion was not merely about separation for its own sake, but about the pursuit of a space where African Americans could worship, learn, and grow without the constraints of racial subjugation. By calling for a religious institution that was uniquely African American, Woodson was laying

237

the groundwork for the broader movements of black empowerment that would emerge in the decades to come.

The work of Reverend Woodson, while lesser known in the mainstream historical narrative, was crucial in shaping the trajectory of African American religious thought and practice. His vision for a self-determined black church would echo throughout the social and political history of African Americans, from the abolitionist movement to the Civil Rights Movement and beyond.

New York Committee of Vigilance: David Ruggles 1836

David Ruggles (March 24, 1810 – 1849) was a tireless and influential abolitionist, activist, and freedom fighter whose work significantly shaped the landscape of the anti-slavery movement in the early 19th century. Born into a world where slavery and racial oppression were deeply entrenched in the United States, Ruggles dedicated his life to fighting for the freedom of enslaved people and promoting equal rights for African Americans. His life and legacy stand as a testament to the power of resilience, courage, and dedication to justice.

As one of the most prominent Black abolitionists of his time, Ruggles played a critical role in the Underground Railroad, helping runaway slaves find freedom in the northern states and beyond. In addition to his work in abolitionism, he was also a staunch advocate for Black self-help, education, and healthcare. His multifaceted contributions to the freedom movement, combined with his pioneering work in promoting Black empowerment, have made him an essential figure in the history of African American activism.

David Ruggles was born in New York City on March 24, 1810, to free Black parents, which was a significant distinction in a nation where slavery still existed in the southern states and racial discrimination was widespread even in the North. He was one of the few free African Americans born in New York during a time when

239

most African Americans in the city were still enslaved. This early experience of freedom shaped Ruggles' worldview, instilling in him a fierce sense of justice and a desire to fight for the freedom of those still enslaved.

Ruggles received an education in New York City, a rarity for Black children at the time, and was deeply influenced by the abolitionist movements he encountered in his youth. He was especially inspired by the activism of prominent abolitionists such as Frederick Douglass, Sojourner Truth, and William Lloyd Garrison. Ruggles' exposure to these influential figures, combined with his own experiences of witnessing the brutality of slavery and racism, galvanized him to become actively involved in the abolitionist cause.

David Ruggles' most significant contribution to the abolitionist movement was his pivotal role in the Underground Railroad—a network of secret routes, safe houses, and individuals dedicated to assisting escaped slaves in their pursuit of freedom. Ruggles became one of the most effective and resourceful conductors on this network, working primarily in New York City, which was a critical transit point for runaway slaves heading north or seeking asylum in Canada. His commitment to the cause and his extraordinary organizing skills made him one of the most well-known figures in the Underground Railroad system.

Ruggles took an active role in housing runaway slaves in New York City and providing them with the means to escape the dangers of capture. His New York-based safe house became a haven for those fleeing from the South. In addition to offering shelter, he helped runaways find jobs, secure passage to the North, and connect with abolitionist networks that would aid them on their journey to freedom. Ruggles was particularly known for his courage in confronting slave catchers and working with other abolitionists to expose the Fugitive Slave Act of 1850, a law that made it even more dangerous for enslaved people to seek freedom in the North.

One of Ruggles' most celebrated achievements was his role in helping Shadrach Minkins, a runaway slave from Virginia, escape from federal authorities in Boston in 1851. Minkins had been arrested under the provisions of the Fugitive Slave Act but was ultimately freed through the collective efforts of abolitionists and Black activists like Ruggles. This event, along with others, cemented Ruggles' reputation as an unwavering defender of freedom and human dignity.

Ruggles was not only an abolitionist; he was also a strong proponent of African American rights in a broader sense. In the 1830s, New York was home to a thriving African American community that was increasingly vocal in its demands for justice, freedom, and equality. Ruggles was an integral part of this community, using his voice to advocate for Black empowerment, self-reliance, and education.

Ruggles believed that the path to true liberation for African Americans was not simply the abolition of slavery, but also the

241

establishment of independent and sustainable communities for free Black people. He advocated for the establishment of Black schools, businesses, and social organizations that would help African Americans build wealth, gain social status, and create an infrastructure that could support their freedom and success.

He was instrumental in organizing the New York Committee of Vigilance, which was dedicated to protecting the rights of Black people, particularly runaway slaves. This group sought to protect Black families from slave catchers and to ensure that Black people in the North were treated with dignity and respect. Ruggles and his fellow abolitionists also pushed for laws that would allow free Black people to vote, gain access to property, and receive an education.

Additionally, Ruggles was a passionate advocate for Black health, particularly the wellbeing of African American families. In the early 19th century, Black communities suffered from both a lack of access to healthcare and institutional racism that prevented them from receiving proper medical care. As an advocate for healthcare access, Ruggles worked tirelessly to promote sanitation, disease prevention, and medical education for African Americans.

One of the defining struggles of Ruggles' life was his opposition to the Fugitive Slave Act of 1850, which required citizens in free states to assist in the capture and return of runaway slaves. The act was a powerful tool in maintaining the institution of slavery and undermining the rights of free Black people in the North. Ruggles and his allies viewed the act as a direct assault on Black freedom and fought it with all the resources at their disposal.

Ruggles himself became a target of slave catchers and law enforcement officials due to his involvement in the Underground Railroad and his outspoken opposition to the Fugitive Slave Act. He was arrested and harassed on several occasions for his efforts to assist runaway slaves. Despite these efforts to silence him, Ruggles remained undeterred, continuing his work as a leader in the abolitionist movement and as a tireless fighter for Black rights.

Though David Ruggles passed away in 1849 at the age of 39, his contributions to the abolitionist movement and to the fight for African American rights continue to be felt today. His legacy is one of courage, commitment, and self-sacrifice in the service of freedom. Ruggles' work in the Underground Railroad and his efforts to support African American communities are a testament to the idea that true freedom requires not just the absence of slavery, but the empowerment of people to live with dignity, independence, and opportunity.

Ruggles' contributions to the fight for Black freedom and equality have been increasingly recognized by historians, though his role has often been overshadowed by more renowned figures like Harriet Tubman and Frederick Douglass. Nevertheless, his efforts were critical in the fight to ensure that African Americans could live free and dignified lives in a society that had long relegated them to the status of second-class citizens.

David Ruggles' life embodies the unwavering spirit of resistance and the enduring fight for freedom. His work with the Underground Railroad, his efforts to secure basic human rights for African Americans, and his dedication to healthcare and education created a foundation for the fight for freedom that would be continued by later generations. Through his actions, Ruggles demonstrated that true abolitionism was not simply about the abolition of slavery—it was about the creation of a world where Black people could live freely, with access to education, economic independence, and equal rights. His legacy continues to inspire generations of activists, educators, and advocates for social justice.

Destiny of the People of Color: James McCune Smith 1841

James McCune Smith, born on April 18, 1813, in New York City, was a man ahead of his time. A physician, abolitionist, and intellectual, McCune Smith's life was a profound testament to the resilience of the human spirit in the face of systemic oppression. His career and writings contributed significantly to the intellectual and social movements of the 19th century, and his legacy remains an essential part of the story of African American empowerment and the struggle for racial equality. As an advocate for the destiny of people of color, McCune Smith used his extraordinary intellect and education to challenge prevailing racist ideologies and argue for a future in which African Americans could fully realize their potential.

McCune Smith was not just any intellectual; he was the first African American to earn a medical degree in the United States, and his work as a physician was as much about healing bodies as it was about changing minds. He was acutely aware of the barriers faced by Black people, both in the United States and abroad, but he believed in the inherent potential of people of color to overcome them. In his time, when white supremacy was woven into the very fabric of society, McCune Smith's voice was one of defiance, a clear refusal to accept the prevailing beliefs about race.

James McCune Smith's early life set the stage for the challenges and triumphs that would

245

define his later years. Born in New York City to parents who were both formerly enslaved, McCune Smith was raised in the North, where slavery had been abolished but racial prejudice was still rampant. Despite the lack of opportunities for Black people in almost every field, McCune Smith showed an early aptitude for learning. Smith was accepted into a public school, where he excelled academically, and soon began to cultivate a thirst for knowledge that would later propel him to become one of the leading intellectual figures of his generation.

However, McCune Smith faced significant challenges. In his youth, he was often denied access to higher education simply because of his race. He applied to several American medical schools but was rejected on the grounds that they did not admit Black students. Undeterred by these obstacles, McCune Smith turned to Europe. In 1837, he enrolled at the University of Glasgow in Scotland, where he earned his medical degree in 1837, becoming the first African American to hold a medical degree.

Upon his return to the United States, McCune Smith faced another form of discrimination. Although he was a trained and qualified physician, many white medical institutions refused to hire him due to his race. Nonetheless, he established a successful medical practice in New York City, where he became a prominent figure within the African American community. His medical career, however, was only one aspect of his broader social mission.

McCune Smith's intellectual contributions to the racial discourse of the 19th century were nothing short of revolutionary. At a time when pseudoscientific theories of racial inferiority were being used to justify slavery and discrimination, McCune Smith firmly rejected these ideas. His work as a physician and his education in Europe equipped him with the tools to engage with and critique the prevailing racial ideologies of his day.

One of his most significant contributions to the conversation about race was his critique of Samuel George Morton's craniometry, a pseudoscientific method that claimed to demonstrate the intellectual inferiority of Black people by measuring skull size. Morton and other proponents of this theory had argued that the physical characteristics of Black people, particularly the size and shape of their skulls, were evidence of their supposed intellectual and moral inferiority. McCune Smith, in his writings, systematically debunked these claims, using empirical evidence and a deep understanding of anatomy and biology to show that Morton's conclusions were not scientifically valid.

In a famous essay, "The Relation of the Negro to the African and to the Caucasian," McCune Smith argued that race was not a biological determinant of intelligence or character, but a social construct used to perpetuate inequality. He examined how racial prejudice had been used to deny opportunities to African Americans, not because of inherent racial differences but because of a deeply entrenched system of racism that sought to justify the status quo of slavery and oppression.

247

In his work, McCune Smith often turned to history to illustrate his points. He looked at the achievements of African civilizations, the contributions of Black people to the world's cultural and scientific advancements, and the remarkable resilience of enslaved Africans who had managed to maintain their dignity and humanity despite the brutal conditions of slavery. These historical examples were intended to challenge the prevailing view of African Americans as inferior and incapable of intellectual, moral, or artistic achievement.

Beyond his work in medicine and racial theory, McCune Smith was deeply committed to the abolitionist movement. He was a frequent contributor to abolitionist publications, including *The Emancipator*, and worked closely with leaders such as Frederick Douglass and Sojourner Truth. McCune Smith understood that the fight for the rights of Black people was not limited to the abolition of slavery but extended to the broader struggle for racial equality and justice in all aspects of life.

He believed that the fate of Black people in America was not to be defined by the system of slavery, nor by the racist ideologies that sought to subordinate them. Instead, he believed that the destiny of people of color lay in their ability to define their own lives, to contribute to society on their own terms, and to gain access to the same rights and opportunities as white Americans. In his writing and speeches, McCune Smith consistently argued that African Americans were just as capable of intellectual, moral, and professional achievement as their white

248

counterparts. His career as a physician was a testament to this belief, as he used his position to challenge both the medical profession's racial biases and the broader societal view of Black people's potential.

McCune Smith also advocated for the full inclusion of African Americans in political life. He believed that Black people should have the right to vote, hold office, and participate fully in American democracy. He was an early advocate for Black suffrage, arguing that the ability to vote was a crucial element of full citizenship and equality. In his view, the denial of the vote to Black men was a fundamental injustice that perpetuated the social and political marginalization of African Americans.

The central theme of James McCune Smith's work was the idea of the "destiny of people of color." For McCune Smith, the future of Black Americans and people of African descent was one of self-determination, intellectual growth, and social equality. He refused to accept the prevailing notion that African Americans were destined to be subordinate to white Americans. Instead, he believed that people of color were capable of achieving greatness in all aspects of life—medicine, the arts, politics, and more.

In his writings, McCune Smith often envisioned a future where racial equality was not just a distant dream but a reality that could be achieved through education, social activism, and the rejection of racial prejudices. His vision of the destiny of people of color was one where Black people were fully integrated into society, with access to education, healthcare, and political rights. He saw the abolition of slavery as only the first step in this process, believing that true freedom would only come when racial discrimination was eradicated and when African Americans were able to realize their full potential.

James McCune Smith's influence extended far beyond his lifetime. His intellectual contributions laid the groundwork for future generations of Black scholars, activists, and intellectuals who would continue to challenge the racial prejudices of American society. His work paved the way for the civil rights movement, the Harlem Renaissance, and the broader struggle for racial equality in the 20th century.

Despite the obstacles he faced as a Black man in a deeply racist society, McCune Smith's life serves as a testament to the power of education, perseverance, and unwavering belief in the dignity and potential of people of color. His advocacy for the destiny of people of color—that they could and should be equal to whites in every aspect of life—remains one of the most enduring messages in the history of American racial thought.

James McCune Smith died on November 17, 1865, but his ideas and legacy live on in the ongoing struggle for racial equality and the fight to ensure that all people, regardless of race, have the opportunity to shape their own destinies.

A Radical Call to Arms & Rebellion: Henry Highland Garnet 1843

Born into the horrors of slavery and rising to prominence as one of the most compelling voices for freedom and abolition, Henry Highland Garnet stands as a monumental figure in the 19th-century fight for Black liberation. His life, as both a freedman and an abolitionist, offers a powerful example of the intellectual and spiritual transformation that would help shape the broader movement toward emancipation. Garnet's journey from an enslaved child to a leading abolitionist orator, minister, and advocate for armed resistance is one that illuminates the complexity and diversity of thought within the movement for Black freedom.

Henry Highland Garnet was born on December 23, 1815, in Kent County, Maryland, to enslaved parents. His early years were defined by the brutal conditions of slavery. His father, Thomas Garnet, was a slave who had been born in Africa, and his mother, Rosa Garnet, was also enslaved. The Garnet family was fortunate to have been able to escape to freedom, but only after experiencing the immense toll of the system of human bondage.

Around the age of nine, Garnet and his family escaped from slavery. The Garnet family fled north to Philadelphia via the Underground Railroad, where they ultimately settled in New York City. The transition from slavery to freedom was not a seamless process, and Henry's

251

experience as a child in bondage left a deep imprint on him. His early exposure to the horrors of slavery shaped his strong commitment to abolition and his later radical views on the need for complete Black liberation.

While living in New York, Garnet was able to attend school and, by 1834, he enrolled in the Oneida Institute in Whitesboro, New York. The Oneida Institute was a progressive institution that catered to both Black and white students, and it became one of the first integrated schools in the country to educate Black students, offering them a foundation in classical studies, theology, and abolitionist thought. Garnet flourished at the Institute and began to develop a passion for activism and intellectual inquiry, making connections with prominent abolitionists.

After completing his education, Garnet became a prominent figure within the African Methodist Episcopal Church (AME), where he was ordained as a minister. His work as a clergyman was deeply intertwined with his abolitionist activities, and he used the pulpit as a platform to denounce slavery and advocate for the rights of African Americans. As a preacher, Garnet was known for his eloquent and impassioned speeches, which blended Christian morality with a call for social justice and the immediate emancipation of enslaved people.

In the 1840s, Garnet's work as both a minister and an abolitionist began to take on a more national scope. He traveled far and wide, delivering speeches and sermons to abolitionist groups across the northern United States, becoming known for his stirring oratorical skills. His speeches often fused elements of religion and radical politics, drawing from both his Christian faith and his desire for social change. Unlike many of his contemporaries, who advocated for gradual emancipation, Garnet was an advocate of immediate abolition—a call that would align him with other radical abolitionists of the time.

However, Garnet's message was more radical than that of many abolitionists. His belief in Black self-reliance, coupled with his opposition to gradualist approaches, eventually led him to embrace more extreme positions, including the use of armed resistance as a means of achieving freedom.

Perhaps Garnet's most famous moment came in 1843, when he delivered his renowned speech, "An Address to the Slaves of the United States." In this powerful oration, Garnet argued that slaves should rise up against their oppressors and fight for their freedom. This was a stark contrast to the mainstream abolitionist movement, which, particularly in the North, was largely committed to nonviolent protest and political action.

In his address, Garnet took an uncompromising stance on slavery. He proclaimed that slavery was an immoral and illegitimate institution and that the enslaved people themselves were the rightful agents of their own liberation. In some of the speech's most radical lines, he exhorted the enslaved to take up arms in defense of their freedom, stating:

"Let your motto be resistance! resistance! resistance! No oppressed people have ever secured their liberty without resistance. The struggle may be long, but it will bring liberty."

This message of resistance, while controversial at the time, was deeply resonant for those who saw peaceful abolition as insufficient to combat the brutal reality of slavery. Garnet's call for armed insurrection also positioned him as a precursor to later figures such as Nat Turner and Harriet Tubman, who would take more militant stands in the fight for freedom.

While Garnet's speech advocating for armed resistance made him a divisive figure in the abolitionist movement, he was still a key player in pushing for emancipation and civil rights. As an abolitionist leader, Garnet worked tirelessly for the eradication of slavery, racial equality, and the rights of African Americans. He was deeply involved in various abolitionist societies and worked closely with other leaders such as Frederick Douglass, Sojourner Truth, and William Lloyd Garrison. His approach, while often more radical, was still firmly rooted in the belief that all people should be free and equal, regardless of race or background.

Garnet also held important leadership positions within the AME Church. In the 1840s, he became one of the leading spokesmen for the church and its advocacy for social justice. He was involved in church politics and worked to create new institutions that would help African Americans transition from slavery to freedom, including schools and organizations dedicated to political activism.

In addition to his work in the abolitionist movement, Garnet was also involved in the repatriation movement, which promoted the idea of returning formerly enslaved Black people to Africa—specifically to Liberia, a nation founded by free Black Americans. While Garnet's views on colonization evolved over time, and he became increasingly critical of it, his early involvement with the idea is a testament to his efforts to secure freedom for African Americans in all forms

After the Civil War and the Emancipation Proclamation of 1863, Henry Highland Garnet's activism did not diminish. As the first Black person to speak before the U.S. House of Representatives in 1865, he addressed Congress on the topic of reparations and the rights of African Americans in the post-war era, pushing for the integration of Black Americans into all facets of American society. Garnet was also an advocate for education and self-determination for newly freed African Americans.

Though he did not live to see the full fruits of his labor—having passed away in 1882—Garnet's work contributed significantly to the intellectual and spiritual underpinnings of the Black liberation movement that would flourish in the 20th century. His speeches, writings, and activism played a foundational role in shaping the arguments for freedom and equality, contributing to the voices of W.E.B. Du Bois, Marcus Garvey, and later civil rights leaders.

Henry Highland Garnet's legacy is complex but undeniably powerful. He was an intellectual, preacher, and activist who took an uncompromising stand for the abolition of slavery and the equality of African Americans. While his call for armed resistance made him a controversial figure in his time, Garnet's commitment to self-liberation, his powerful rhetoric, and his actions in support of African American rights remain integral to the history of the abolitionist movement and the struggle for Black freedom.

His words, particularly in the 1843 address to the enslaved, continue to resonate as a call for resistance against oppression. As one of the earliest figures to advocate for Black self-determination, Henry Highland Garnet occupies a vital place in the long history of Black activism, and his contributions were instrumental in shaping the abolitionist cause and the broader fight for racial justice.

The Father of Black Nationalism & The North Star: Martin Delaney 1847

Martin Delaney (1812–1885) was a pioneering figure in American history, an abolitionist, a physician, and one of the most vocal advocates for Black empowerment during the 19th century. His life and work intersected with many key movements of the era, from the abolition of slavery to the early efforts for Black political and social independence. In a time when African Americans were often confined to a narrative of oppression and victimhood, Delaney's words and deeds challenged both the status quo and the prevailing attitudes toward race in America.

Martin Delaney was born in Charles Town, Virginia (now part of West Virginia), in 1812, into a world that had little hope for the advancement of Black people. His mother, a free Black woman, and his father, who was enslaved but later freed, helped instill in him a strong sense of self-worth and determination. He was one of the few to be literate as a child, thanks to his mother's efforts and the support of free Black communities that valued education.

Delaney's early life was marked by his keen intelligence and a desire to learn, yet he faced constant racial barriers. In his youth, he witnessed the harsh realities of slavery and the extreme discrimination that Black people endured in both the South and the North. These

257

experiences would deeply shape his views and guide his life's work.

Despite the constraints of the time, Delaney pursued education, attending the African Free School in Pittsburgh, Pennsylvania, where he worked under the mentorship of a local abolitionist. After moving to Pittsburgh in the early 1830s, Delaney's interests expanded from reading and writing to medicine. In 1838, he began studying to become a physician, but the challenges he faced in gaining access to medical schools due to his race were daunting.

Delaney's first major step onto the public stage came in the 1840s when he became involved in the abolitionist movement. He was part of a group of radical Black thinkers who rejected the idea that African Americans should passively await emancipation or integration into white society. He became deeply involved in the *National Negro Convention* and was a vocal advocate for immediate abolition and Black self-sufficiency.

Delaney also worked closely with prominent abolitionists like Frederick Douglass, although their relationship was sometimes strained. While both men sought the abolition of slavery, Delaney was often more radical in his views, arguing that Black people needed to take control of their own destinies, both in the context of slavery and in the post-emancipation world. Delaney argued for Black self-defense, Black political power, and the importance of Black identity, at a time when many abolitionists

believed that Black people needed to assimilate
into white society.

Delaney's views often stood in contrast to
those of Douglass, who believed in a gradual path
to equality and integration. Delaney, on the other
hand, pushed for more immediate action and
more radical steps. He believed that African
Americans should resist all forms of subjugation
and should aim for a fully realized identity
outside of white society. This was reflected in his
emphasis on the importance of Black self-help
institutions, self-education, and political
mobilization.

One of the most controversial aspects of
Delaney's activism was his support for
emigration. In the mid-19th century, Delaney
began to advocate for the emigration of Black
people to Africa. He believed that African
Americans, especially those who had been born
into slavery or were born under the oppressive
system of racism, could never truly find equality
or peace in America. Delaney's solution was not
to integrate into white society but to build an
independent Black nation in Africa.

In the 1850s, Delaney toured parts of
Africa, most notably Liberia, as part of his effort
to explore the possibilities of colonization. He was
particularly interested in finding a place where
African Americans could establish their own
communities, free from the systemic racism that
poisoned American society. His interest in
emigration, however, was not simply about
escape; he saw it as a form of empowerment. For
Delaney, it was not about rejecting American

259

culture but creating an alternative that could provide freedom, autonomy, and self-respect for Black people.

While many African Americans, including Douglass, rejected emigration as an unrealistic and divisive solution, Delaney's advocacy for it revealed his deep dissatisfaction with the prospects of equality within the United States. His vision of a Black diaspora was not one of exile but of opportunity, a chance for a new world where Black people could define their futures on their own terms.

Delaney was also one of the first Black physicians in America, earning his medical degree in 1854 from the Pennsylvania Medical University. In the era before the Civil War, when Black people were excluded from mainstream institutions, this was a remarkable achievement. However, Delaney's medical work extended beyond just treating patients; it was closely tied to his activism.

Delaney viewed medicine as a means to empower Black people by promoting health and wellness within their own communities. He became a fierce advocate for the health of Black people, particularly Black women and children. Delaney's approach to medicine was not just about individual treatment but about social and public health. He understood that the health of Black people could not be separated from the larger social and political struggles they faced.

His medical work was also deeply connected to his racial consciousness. Delaney was one of the few Black doctors to challenge the notion that African Americans were inherently inferior or more prone to disease. He pushed back against the pseudoscientific ideas of race that permeated American medicine and argued that health disparities were the result of social conditions rather than biological differences.

When the Civil War broke out, Delaney became one of the most vocal proponents for the inclusion of Black soldiers in the Union Army. He believed that the war was not only a struggle to end slavery but a fight for Black empowerment. Delaney was a strong supporter of Black military service, seeing it as an essential part of the Black struggle for freedom. He pushed for the recruitment of Black soldiers, and he was appointed by President Abraham Lincoln as the first Black field officer in the U.S. Army.

Despite his accomplishments, Delaney faced significant obstacles within the military. The Union Army was often reluctant to fully embrace Black soldiers, and Delaney himself was sometimes frustrated by the slow pace of change. His leadership in organizing and advocating for Black troops left a lasting legacy, and the experience of Black soldiers in the Civil War helped lay the groundwork for future struggles for civil rights and political equality.

After the Civil War, Delaney continued his work in the Black community, though his later years were marked by personal struggles and financial hardship. He worked as a physician, writer, and editor but was largely marginalized from the mainstream political discourse of

261

Reconstruction. He did, however, continue to advocate for the political and social rights of Black people, and his writings, particularly his book *The Condition, Elevation, Emigration, and Destiny of the Colored People of the United States* (1852), remained important contributions to the broader discourse on Black empowerment.

Martin Delaney's impact on the Black liberation movement cannot be overstated. His efforts to uplift Black people through self-reliance, self-defense, education, and emigration were bold and uncompromising. He was a radical thinker who believed in the full equality of Black people but also recognized that true freedom might only be achieved through radical action and self-determination.

Delaney's legacy as a physician, abolitionist, and political leader set the stage for future generations of Black leaders, from Booker T. Washington to W.E.B. Du Bois and beyond. His vision for a liberated and empowered Black people, unafraid to demand their rightful place in the world, continues to resonate in the ongoing struggles for racial justice today.

The Father of the Underground Railroad: William Still 1848

William Still (October 7, 1821 – July 14, 1902) was one of the most prominent and impactful figures in the Underground Railroad, the network of secret routes and safe houses that helped thousands of enslaved African Americans escape to freedom in the North and Canada. Known as the "Father of the Underground Railroad," Still's legacy is intertwined with his tireless work to assist fugitive slaves, his meticulous record-keeping, and his leadership in the abolitionist movement. His life and contributions provide a powerful narrative of courage, compassion, and steadfast commitment to freedom.

Still's role as an administrator, organizer, and chronicler of the Underground Railroad makes him one of the most important and effective agents of Black resistance to slavery. He not only provided vital assistance to runaway slaves but also worked to document their stories—preserving the personal accounts of freedom seekers for posterity. This chapter will explore William Still's early life, his work in the Underground Railroad, and his lasting influence on the history of abolitionism and African American self-determination.

William Still was born in Chellow, New Jersey, in 1821 to Charles Still, a free African American, and Nancy (Hancock) Still, who was born enslaved in Maryland but later gained her freedom. As a child, Still moved with his family to

263

Philadelphia, which, at the time, was a vibrant center for abolitionism and home to many prominent figures in the fight against slavery. In Philadelphia, Still received an education, though it was limited by racial prejudice. Despite the challenges, Still was determined to improve his circumstances and pursue a life of activism.

As a young man, Still worked various jobs, including as a waiter, and later as a clerk at the Pennsylvania Anti-Slavery Society. His exposure to the abolitionist movement in Philadelphia played a crucial role in shaping his future work. He became close to many of the city's leading abolitionists, including Lucretia Mott and Thomas Garrett, and learned from their example of resistance and organizing. Still's work in the abolitionist cause was not just about rhetoric or ideology; he took practical, hands-on action to help escapees and stand against the institution of slavery.

In the 1850s, Still's life would become forever connected to the Underground Railroad, the clandestine network of people and routes that helped fugitive slaves make their way to freedom. Although the railroad was made up of many different stations and conductors, William Still was one of the most organized and determined leaders in the effort. His role was multifaceted: he provided logistical support, communicated with other abolitionists, and served as a liaison between the fugitive slaves and their final destination—often Canada.

Still became one of the most prominent station masters in Philadelphia, a key city on the

Underground Railroad. At his home, Still harbored and cared for fugitive slaves, helping them stay safe while they made arrangements for the next leg of their journey. He often worked closely with other conductors, like Harriet Tubman, to make sure the enslaved people could escape without detection. Still used his network of trusted allies—both Black and white abolitionists—to ensure that the escapees were cared for until they were ready to continue their journey north.

One of Still's most notable contributions was his systematic record-keeping. Unlike many other conductors, Still meticulously documented the names, physical descriptions, and personal stories of the people he helped escape. These records provided invaluable first-hand accounts of the experiences of the fugitive slaves and became part of the foundation for Black history. They were also critical in the broader abolitionist struggle, as they demonstrated the widespread brutality of slavery and the courage of those who sought freedom. His records were later published in his book, "The Underground Railroad: A Record of Facts, Authentic Narratives, Letters, &c.", which remains a key primary source on the Underground Railroad.

Still's records also helped reunite families that had been torn apart by slavery. On several occasions, Still was able to track down family members who had been separated during their escape and reconnect them. His work was not just about helping people escape slavery but about preserving the dignity and humanity of those who had suffered under it. The freedom he

265

provided was not only a physical escape from captivity but also a form of emotional and psychological healing.

Working on the Underground Railroad was extraordinarily dangerous. Enslaved individuals, as well as the abolitionists who helped them, risked capture, punishment, and even death if caught. The Fugitive Slave Act of 1850 heightened the risks for everyone involved, as it required runaway slaves to be returned to their enslavers, even if they had reached free states. The law also penalized anyone who assisted a fugitive slave, making it a crime to shelter, feed, or transport escapees.

Despite these grave dangers, Still remained committed to the cause of freedom. He was aware of the risks but chose to stand firm in his efforts to aid the oppressed. His home was often a target for bounty hunters, and Still had to be incredibly cautious to ensure that his activities went undetected. Still's ability to navigate these dangers without being caught was a testament to his resourcefulness, his faith, and his network of loyal supporters.

The fear of betrayal was also a constant threat. It was not uncommon for runaway slaves to be turned in for money, or for information to leak to authorities. Still's meticulous care in selecting and vetting individuals was a crucial component of his success. He carefully cultivated a circle of trusted allies, both Black and white, who shared his commitment to the abolitionist cause and would never betray the fugitives in their care.

After the Civil War ended in 1865 and slavery was abolished, Still continued his work as an advocate for African American rights. He became involved in civil rights efforts and was a strong supporter of Black suffrage. Still was one of the founding members of the Pennsylvania Anti-Slavery Society, and after the war, he worked with other Black leaders to ensure that African Americans received the full rights and protections afforded by the 13th, 14th, and 15th Amendments.

Still was also active in efforts to promote the education of African Americans, establishing schools for freedmen and advocating for more educational opportunities for Black children. His own family was a significant part of his legacy; his children carried on the work of their father in their own ways, furthering the cause of freedom, equality, and justice for African Americans.

William Still passed away on July 14, 1902, leaving behind a profound legacy as one of the most important and effective leaders of the Underground Railroad. His records and testimonies have remained vital in understanding the history of slavery and the abolitionist movement in the United States. His book, *The Underground Railroad: A Record of Facts*, is considered an essential work for historians, researchers, and anyone interested in the history of Black resistance to slavery.

William Still's contribution to the abolition of slavery and the freedom of enslaved African Americans cannot be overstated. As a leader, conductor, and chronicler, Still's work helped

267

bring thousands of people to safety. His careful documentation of their stories preserved their histories and has allowed us to understand the personal and collective struggles of those who sought freedom. Still's unflinching commitment to the cause of liberty, justice, and human dignity remains an inspiration to those fighting for equality and freedom today. His life exemplifies the power of individual action in the fight against injustice, and his legacy is woven into the fabric of the freedom struggle in America.

The Hayden House of the Underground Railroad: Lewis Hayden 1849

Lewis Hayden, born into enslavement in 1811, is remembered as one of the most courageous and tenacious abolitionists of the 19th century. His life spanned the critical period in American history when slavery was entrenched in the South, abolitionism was gaining momentum in the North, and the struggle for freedom reached its boiling point. Hayden's journey from slavery to freedom, and from fugitive to outspoken leader, exemplifies the spirit of resistance that defined the abolitionist movement.

Lewis Hayden was born in 1811 in Lexington, Kentucky, to enslaved parents. Kentucky was a border state, situated between the free states of the North and the slave states of the South, and as such, it represented a crossroads of sorts—caught between two conflicting worlds. As a young man, Hayden was subjected to the harsh realities of slavery, working on a plantation under the brutal authority of his enslavers. Although he never knew the full extent of his family's history, it is clear that Hayden, like many enslaved people, was driven by an intense desire for freedom.

In his early adulthood, Hayden was sold to a man named James D. Wade, a notoriously cruel slaveholder. Under Wade's ownership, Hayden was subjected to even more dehumanizing conditions, and his desire to escape grew

269

stronger. In 1844, when he was in his early thirties, Hayden made the fateful decision to flee. With the help of a network of abolitionists and sympathetic free Black people, Hayden escaped northward, navigating the perilous journey of the Underground Railroad. He found his way to Cincinnati, Ohio, and later to Detroit, Michigan, where he crossed into Canada and secured his freedom.

Though he was physically free in Canada, Hayden's desire to fight against slavery and contribute to the cause of Black liberation would not allow him to remain on the sidelines. He quickly became a vocal advocate for abolition, devoting himself to the cause of freedom and the liberation of others still trapped in the chains of slavery.

After gaining his freedom in Canada, Hayden moved to Boston, a center of abolitionist activity in the United States. Boston had long been a hotbed for anti-slavery sentiment, and it was there that Hayden would make his most significant contributions to the abolitionist movement. Upon arriving, he joined the vibrant and growing network of abolitionists, including figures like William Lloyd Garrison, Frederick Douglass, and Harriet Beecher Stowe, who were all fighting for the end of slavery.

One of the most important aspects of Hayden's work was his involvement with the Underground Railroad, the secret network of safe houses, routes, and people who helped enslaved individuals escape to free states and Canada. Hayden himself had benefitted from this network

270

during his own escape, and now, as a free man, he became an active part of it. Along with his wife, Harriet, and other abolitionists, he assisted numerous enslaved people on their journeys to freedom. Hayden's house in Boston became a station on the Underground Railroad, providing shelter and food for those fleeing enslavement.

His commitment to the Underground Railroad was not without danger. Those who helped slaves to escape could face imprisonment or even death. Hayden was well aware of the risk, but he refused to back down. He became one of the most prominent Black abolitionists in Boston, delivering speeches and participating in protests, advocating for the abolition of slavery, and supporting the rights of Black people in the North.

The passage of the Fugitive Slave Act of 1850 was a direct challenge to everything Hayden stood for. The law made it legally permissible for slave catchers to go into free states and capture escaped slaves, who would then be returned to their owners in the South. It also imposed harsh penalties on anyone who aided runaway slaves. Hayden was one of the first to take action against the law.

In 1851, when a fugitive named Shadrach Minkins was apprehended in Boston and threatened with being returned to slavery in the South, Hayden and other abolitionists took decisive action. Minkins had escaped from Virginia, and when he was captured, he was locked up in a Boston courtroom to await extradition. As the case progressed, abolitionists

271

and Black activists in the city organized a bold rescue operation. Hayden and his fellow abolitionists stormed the courthouse, freeing Minkins and escorting him to Canada, where he could live as a free man.

This bold act of resistance was a defining moment in Hayden's life, as well as in the larger abolitionist movement. The successful rescue of Minkins helped to galvanize opposition to the Fugitive Slave Act, and it demonstrated to the nation that the abolitionists would not stand idly by while the federal government enforced laws that violated the rights and freedoms of Black people.

In addition to his work on the Underground Railroad, Lewis Hayden became a leader in the African American community in Boston. He was active in the Massachusetts Anti-Slavery Society and helped organize protests and rallies. He was a skilled orator, known for his passionate speeches about liberty, justice, and the rights of Black people. He also worked closely with other prominent abolitionists, including Frederick Douglass, and Sojourner Truth, lending his voice and leadership to the cause of emancipation.

Hayden's activism also extended beyond the abolition of slavery. He was a strong proponent of education for Black people, recognizing that education was a vital tool for Black empowerment and self-liberation. He worked with local schools and institutions to promote the education of Black children and adults, believing that the fight for freedom could

272

not be won without the intellectual and cultural advancement of Black people.

As the nation moved toward the Civil War in the 1860s, Hayden's role as an abolitionist became even more vital. The Civil War was, in many ways, a culmination of the sectional conflicts between the North and South, especially over the issue of slavery. Hayden, like many abolitionists, supported the Union's efforts to defeat the Confederacy, seeing the war as a crucial moment in the fight to end slavery once and for all.

During the war, Hayden continued to work closely with other Black leaders and abolitionists, lobbying for the inclusion of Black soldiers in the Union Army. He believed that the war was not only a battle to preserve the Union, but also a struggle for the freedom and equality of Black people. Hayden's advocacy helped ensure that Black troops were allowed to fight, and by the end of the war, thousands of Black soldiers had served in the Union Army.

When President Abraham Lincoln issued the Emancipation Proclamation in 1863, declaring all enslaved people in the Confederate states to be free, Hayden celebrated the victory, but he knew that the battle for full equality was far from over. Despite his own freedom and success, Hayden continued to fight for the rights of all Black people, advocating for equal rights, voting rights, and access to education.

After the Civil War, Lewis Hayden remained a prominent figure in the fight for Black rights.

273

He continued to advocate for racial justice, working tirelessly to improve the lives of freed people in the post-war South. He spent the rest of his life pushing for full integration, equality under the law, and protection for Black citizens in the face of growing racial discrimination and violence, especially in the Reconstruction era.

Hayden passed away in 1889, leaving behind a legacy of courage, perseverance, and commitment to the cause of liberty. His life as an abolitionist, his involvement in the Underground Railroad, and his leadership in Boston's Black community are a testament to the strength and resilience of Black Americans during one of the most tumultuous periods in U.S. history. Though he is often overshadowed by other more famous abolitionists, Lewis Hayden's contributions to the cause of freedom should never be forgotten.

In the fight against slavery, Hayden was not just an individual, but a symbol of resistance. His bravery helped to pave the way for future generations of activists and leaders, and his legacy endures in the ongoing struggle for racial justice and equality in America.

What to the Slave is the Fourth of July? Frederick Douglass 1852

Frederick Douglass (1818–1895) is one of the most towering figures in American history—an icon of the abolitionist movement, a champion of human rights, and a tireless advocate for the dignity and freedom of Black Americans. His life and work transcend the struggles of his time, offering a vision of justice, equality, and liberty that continues to resonate today. Born into slavery, Douglass became a renowned orator, writer, and statesman, using his experiences of enslavement as a foundation for his fierce advocacy for the abolition of slavery and the full civil rights of African Americans.

Douglass' remarkable journey—from a slave on a Maryland plantation to an internationally recognized leader and statesman—was not only a testament to his intellectual and emotional resilience but also to his belief in the transformative power of education, self-determination, and collective struggle. His eloquence, moral clarity, and courage in speaking truth to power made him one of the most important and influential figures of the 19th century. His speeches, writings, and activism laid the groundwork for future generations of civil rights leaders and remain vital to understanding the ongoing fight for racial justice in America.

Frederick Augustus Washington Bailey was born in February 1818, on the Eastern Shore of Maryland, into slavery. His mother, Harriet

275

Bailey, was enslaved, while his father was likely a white man, though Douglass was never certain of his identity. Douglass spent much of his early childhood apart from his mother, who was forced to work on a different plantation. Separated from his family and isolated in his early years, Douglass' story began with the deep emotional and physical trauma of slavery.

As a child, Douglass was sent to live with the Auld family in Baltimore. It was there, under the influence of Sophia Auld, the wife of his owner, that Douglass first encountered the power of reading and writing. Sophia Auld, despite being a slaveholder, initially taught Douglass the alphabet, but her husband forbade it, believing that educating a slave would make them unmanageable. Undeterred, Douglass took it upon himself to learn to read and write, first by befriending poor white children in the streets and later by sneaking books and materials whenever he could.

Douglass would later write about this transformative moment in his life: "Once you learn to read, you will be forever free."

This early education became Douglass' weapon of resistance. It was through reading that he first encountered ideas about liberty, freedom, and the rights of man, which would help shape his future as one of the most influential abolitionists in American history.

In 1838, at the age of 20, Douglass made the fateful decision to escape from slavery. After years of enduring brutal labor and witnessing the cruel reality of enslavement, he realized that his only hope for freedom lay in escape. With the help of the Underground Railroad and his own determination, Douglass fled to the North, eventually reaching New Bedford, Massachusetts, where he adopted the name "Frederick Douglass" (a name inspired by a character in Sir Walter Scott's poem *The Lady of the Lake*).

Douglass' escape from slavery was not only a personal triumph, but it also set the stage for his later activism. Upon his arrival in the North, Douglass immersed himself in the abolitionist movement. He joined the Anti-Slavery Society and quickly became one of its most prominent speakers. His ability to speak powerfully about his own experiences as a slave made him a highly effective advocate for the abolition of slavery.

Douglass' eloquence and moral authority were key to his success as an abolitionist. He believed that the moral power of his own story— of being born into slavery and rising to freedom— was a compelling argument against the institution of slavery itself. He wrote:

"I didn't know I was a slave until I found out I couldn't do the things I wanted."

Douglass' life as an enslaved man, paired with his intellectual rigor and ability to articulate the horrors of slavery, made him an extraordinary spokesperson for the abolitionist cause. He gave speeches across the Northern United States and even abroad, urging people to see slavery as not only a moral blight but a direct assault on human dignity and the principles of democracy.

277

Douglass' autobiography, *Narrative of the Life of Frederick Douglass, an American Slave*, published in 1845, was a defining moment in his life and in the abolitionist movement. The narrative not only told the story of Douglass' life as a slave and his eventual escape to freedom, but it also served as a powerful indictment of the institution of slavery itself. The book was widely read and became a cornerstone of the abolitionist movement.

In *Narrative*, Douglass detailed the physical and psychological brutality of slavery, describing the severe punishments inflicted on slaves, the degradation of family bonds, and the constant denial of basic human rights. He wrote about how slaveholders manipulated and corrupted both slaves and free people, shaping the social and economic fabric of the nation in ways that violated the principles of justice and equality.

One of the most compelling aspects of Douglass' writing is his analysis of the dehumanizing effects of slavery—not just on slaves, but also on those who held power over them. He often described slavery as a moral disease that corrupted both the victim and the perpetrator, reinforcing the idea that slavery was not merely a social or economic institution, but a profound moral injustice that needed to be eradicated.

Douglass' *Narrative* was a best-seller and brought him fame, but it also caused considerable danger. Douglass' detailed account of the brutality he had witnessed and suffered made him a target for slaveholders and pro-

278

slavery advocates. It also led to increased calls for his capture and re-enslavement, and Douglass was forced to flee to England for a time, where he continued his work as an abolitionist.

Douglass' influence as an abolitionist leader continued to grow throughout the 1840s and 1850s. He worked closely with key abolitionists such as William Lloyd Garrison, but he also became increasingly independent and at times critical of the mainstream abolitionist movement. Douglass believed that the movement was too focused on moral suasion—convincing people to oppose slavery through moral arguments—and not enough on political action. He believed that only through direct political action, including the use of government power to abolish slavery, could the institution be truly eradicated.

Douglass also advocated for the inclusion of women in the abolitionist movement. In 1848, he attended the Seneca Falls Convention, the first women's rights convention in the United States, where he spoke in favor of women's suffrage. Douglass recognized that the struggle for racial justice and gender equality were interconnected and must be fought together.

With the outbreak of the Civil War in 1861, Douglass became a staunch supporter of the Union and used his influence to press President Abraham Lincoln to take stronger action against slavery. Douglass was a firm believer that the war was not only about preserving the Union but also about achieving freedom for Black Americans. He played a key role in recruiting Black soldiers for the Union Army, believing that their participation in the war would not only help win the fight but would also demonstrate the loyalty and bravery of African Americans.

Following the Civil War and the passage of the Thirteenth Amendment, which abolished slavery, Douglass continued to advocate for the rights of freedmen. He fought for the passage of the Fourteenth and Fifteenth Amendments, which granted citizenship and voting rights to African Americans. He also became a prominent voice in the struggle for women's rights and worked for equal treatment for both races and genders during the Reconstruction period.

Douglass continued to speak out against racial inequality and injustice during his later years. He held several important government positions, including U.S. Marshal for the District of Columbia and U.S. Minister to Haiti, and he remained an outspoken critic of racial discrimination in the North and South.

Despite the progress that had been made during Reconstruction, Douglass was disheartened by the persistence of racism and the rise of Jim Crow laws in the post-Reconstruction South. He recognized that the work of achieving true equality for Black Americans was far from over.

Frederick Douglass passed away on February 20, 1895, but his legacy remains one of the most enduring in American history. His life's work—his fight for the abolition of slavery, his advocacy for the rights of women, and his unwavering commitment to equality and justice—shaped the course of American history and continues to influence the struggle for racial justice today.

Douglass taught us that freedom is not just the absence of enslavement but the active realization of human dignity, education, and self-determination. His words, written and spoken, were a clarion call to action, urging Americans to live up to the ideals of liberty and justice upon which the nation was founded.

Douglass' life story is a testament to the transformative power of education and personal agency. From a slave's birth on a Maryland plantation to his stature as an intellectual giant and global human rights advocate, Douglass proved that individuals could not only overcome the brutal circumstances of their birth but also change the course of history.

Today, as we continue to confront issues of racial inequality, police brutality, and the legacy of slavery, Frederick Douglass' words and actions offer both inspiration and a blueprint for the ongoing fight for justice, freedom, and equality.

Daniel Alexander Payne and Wilberforce University in 1856

Daniel Alexander Payne (1811–1893) stands as one of the most significant figures in 19th-century African American history. A scholar, church leader, and advocate for African American rights, Payne played a pivotal role in shaping African American education during a period when both formal schooling and civil rights were often denied to Black people in the United States. His involvement with Wilberforce University in Ohio, founded in 1856, marks a critical point in his career and in the history of African American higher education.

In this chapter, we explore Payne's leadership and his central role in the development of Wilberforce University during its formative years. Wilberforce, as the first private historically Black university in the United States, symbolized the intersection of the religious, intellectual, and political aspirations of African Americans in the mid-19th century. Payne's work at Wilberforce University reflects the larger struggle for Black education and equality in a nation on the brink of civil war.

Daniel Alexander Payne was born on February 24, 1811, in Charleston, South Carolina, to free Black parents. Growing up in a society where enslaved people vastly outnumbered free Black people, Payne was acutely aware of the racial divisions that shaped his world. He was fortunate to receive an education, which was uncommon for Black

282

children in the early 19th century. Payne's thirst for knowledge drove him to pursue academic studies despite the pervasive barriers faced by African Americans.

At the age of 15, Payne left South Carolina for Pennsylvania to attend the Allegheny Institute in Pittsburgh. It was there that he began to develop his deep passion for learning, particularly in the areas of religion, education, and leadership. He later pursued theological studies, which would inform his later work in both the church and in African American education.

In the early 1830s, Payne became a minister in the African Methodist Episcopal Church (AME), an institution that was formed to offer religious leadership to African Americans excluded from predominantly white denominations. As a clergyman and leader within the AME Church, Payne would eventually combine his religious calling with his commitment to advancing the cause of education for African Americans.

Wilberforce University was founded in 1856, and its creation was tied to the mission of the AME Church, which recognized the critical need for higher education among African Americans. The church believed that the intellectual and moral uplift of African Americans was essential for their full participation in American society and their emancipation from both slavery and racial subjugation.

Named after the famous English abolitionist William Wilberforce, the university was established by a group of AME Church leaders who saw education as a means of combating the racial inequality and injustice African Americans faced. The founders envisioned Wilberforce University as an institution that would not only educate Black men and women but would also provide leadership training for the next generation of Black clergy, educators, and activists.

Wilberforce was unique in that it aimed to provide a comprehensive education to African Americans at a time when most Black people had little access to formal schooling. In the mid-19th century, the prevailing educational climate for African Americans was bleak, especially in the Southern states, where laws were passed to prevent the education of enslaved people. In the Northern states, educational opportunities were limited, often relegating Black students to inferior schools with inadequate resources.

Payne's involvement with Wilberforce University began in 1856, when the university was officially chartered. At the time, he was already a prominent leader in the AME Church, having risen through the ranks and eventually becoming the Bishop of the church. His religious standing and his advocacy for education positioned him as a natural leader for the new institution.

Daniel Alexander Payne's vision for Wilberforce University was rooted in his deep belief that education was the key to unlocking African Americans' potential. He recognized that, in a society where racism and inequality were entrenched, African Americans needed more than just basic education. They needed access to higher learning, to intellectual and moral development, and to the tools necessary to challenge the systems of oppression that constrained their lives.

Payne became the university's first president in 1856, and under his leadership, the university focused on providing an academically rigorous and religiously grounded education for African Americans. Payne's experience as an educator and church leader informed the university's early curricula, which blended classical education, religious studies, and practical vocational training. He believed that education should not only address the mind but also the spirit, preparing students to lead both in their communities and in the broader national struggle for equality.

During the early years of Wilberforce University, Payne worked tirelessly to establish the institution's academic reputation and financial stability. Although the university faced numerous challenges—ranging from limited funding to racial prejudices that devalued Black education—Payne was instrumental in building the foundation of what would become a lasting institution of African American higher learning.

Under Payne's leadership, Wilberforce University quickly became a hub for the intellectual and religious advancement of African Americans. As president, Payne oversaw the establishment of key academic programs in subjects such as theology, education, and the

285

arts, with an emphasis on preparing African American students to become leaders in their communities and the church. His emphasis on creating a broad, humanistic education set Wilberforce apart from other institutions of the time, which often focused more narrowly on vocational training.

Despite Payne's leadership, the early years of Wilberforce University were fraught with challenges. In addition to the financial difficulties that all new institutions face, Wilberforce had to contend with the pervasive racism and skepticism about the capabilities of African Americans, both in the broader society and in the religious communities that were critical to the university's support.

Payne's commitment to academic excellence and his insistence on treating African American students with dignity and respect were constant sources of friction with those who believed that Black people were incapable of higher learning. Payne's own tireless work to advocate for Black intellectual and moral equality was met with resistance from both white supremacist forces and from those within the Black community who were skeptical of such ambitious educational goals.

Additionally, the political and social climate of the mid-19th century posed obstacles to Payne's mission. In the decade leading up to the Civil War, tensions between pro-slavery and abolitionist forces were at a fever pitch. The education of African Americans was seen as a direct challenge to the institution of slavery, and

286

many Southern states passed laws prohibiting the education of enslaved people, while Northern states remained deeply divided on the issue of racial equality. Payne's work at Wilberforce University was therefore part of the larger struggle for Black liberation in a nation that was on the brink of civil war.

Despite these challenges, Payne's leadership helped to ensure that Wilberforce remained open and relevant. His commitment to building a strong educational foundation for African Americans in a time of social upheaval helped to lay the groundwork for future generations of Black scholars, leaders, and activists.

By 1856, when Wilberforce University was founded, the landscape of African American education was shifting. While many Black Americans still lacked access to formal schooling, the creation of Wilberforce University represented a major leap forward. It symbolized the growing recognition of the need for institutions of higher learning specifically for African Americans.

Wilberforce University would go on to become a central player in the development of Black education in the United States, particularly after the Civil War, when the Reconstruction Era ushered in new opportunities for Black Americans. Payne's vision for an educated and empowered Black population—able to navigate both the spiritual and secular realms of society—became a cornerstone for the development of African American colleges and universities.

Daniel Alexander Payne's leadership at Wilberforce University in 1856 remains a defining moment in the history of African American education. Payne's relentless belief in the power of education as a tool for Black empowerment and freedom shaped the institution and laid the groundwork for the future of Black higher education in the United States.

The university that Payne helped to establish continues to thrive today, serving as a testament to his commitment to African American progress through learning and leadership. His work not only transformed Wilberforce University but also contributed to the larger narrative of African American resilience, intellectual pursuit, and civic engagement during a time of profound national struggle.

Fifteen-hundred Souls: Jermain Wesley Loguen 1859

Jermain Wesley Loguen was not merely a man of his time; he was a man ahead of it, whose actions and convictions would leave an indelible mark on the abolitionist movement and the fight for human rights. Born a slave in 1813 in Tennessee, Loguen would become one of the most daring and determined freedom fighters of the 19th century, leveraging both his intellect and courage to resist the forces of slavery and racial oppression. His story is one of courage, transformation, and relentless dedication to the cause of liberty.

Jermain Loguen was born into slavery in 1813 in the small town of Tennessee. His birth name was Jerry Loguen, and his early years were marked by the brutal realities of the South's system of enslavement. His mother was also enslaved, and his father's identity remains unclear, though Loguen later claimed his father was a free man of color, a detail that may have shaped his later activism and belief in the capacity for African Americans to live as free men and women.

As a child, Loguen experienced the harshness of slavery firsthand, working in the fields and enduring physical punishment. However, Loguen's intelligence and resourcefulness soon set him apart from the other enslaved people. By his teenage years, he had already learned to read and write, a skill that would prove invaluable in his quest for freedom.

289

He was able to listen to stories about freedom and dreams of escape from those around him, particularly from a friend and fellow enslaved person, Henry "Doc" Hayes, who would later be instrumental in his eventual flight from bondage.

In 1827, Loguen made a daring decision: he escaped from his enslaver. With the help of his mother and others who supported his plan, he managed to make his way to freedom in Canada. At the age of 14, he found himself living in the northern states, first in New York and later in Ohio, where he was free from enslavement. Freedom, however, was not enough for Loguen.

Loguen quickly became involved in the abolitionist movement, using his newfound freedom as a platform to speak out against slavery and fight for its abolition. He was particularly drawn to the growing network of resistance known as the Underground Railroad, a system of secret routes, safe houses, and sympathetic individuals that helped enslaved people escape to the northern states or Canada. Loguen became one of the most active and skilled conductors on this railroad, guiding scores of enslaved people to safety.

Over the years, Loguen's underground work would lead him to establish a network of safe houses, where he harbored and protected runaway slaves. His role in the Underground Railroad was crucial because of his bravery and his deep knowledge of both slave-catchers' tactics and the geography of the Southern United States. Through his actions, Loguen saved hundreds of people, showing courage in the face of great

290

danger. Each time an enslaved person reached the safety of the Northern states, they owed their freedom to his risk-taking and meticulous planning.

Loguen's commitment to abolitionism also included his work as a writer and orator. He wrote extensively about his experiences, documenting his life as both a former enslaved man and an abolitionist leader. In his autobiography, *"The Rev. Jermain Wesley Loguen: His Story, with Remarks on Slavery and Abolition,"* published in 1859, Loguen vividly chronicled his experiences in slavery, his escape, and his subsequent work in the Underground Railroad. His eloquent writing inspired many in the abolitionist movement and cemented his role as one of its most revered leaders.

Beyond his work as an abolitionist, Loguen was also a preacher. His religious beliefs were central to his worldview, and he saw his fight against slavery as a moral imperative. In 1840, he became a minister in the African Methodist Episcopal Zion Church (AME Zion Church), which had long been a haven for free Black people and a center of resistance to the forces of white supremacy. Loguen was an influential figure within the church, and his sermons often focused on themes of liberation and justice.

His leadership extended far beyond his religious duties. Loguen was an advocate for the rights of free Black people, fighting not just for the emancipation of enslaved individuals but also for the equal treatment of free African Americans in the North. He was outspoken against

291

segregation, discrimination, and the violence faced by Black people in the North. At the time, even in free states like New York, African Americans were often denied basic rights, such as access to quality education, employment, and political representation. Loguen, in addition to his work with the Underground Railroad, lobbied for the abolition of discriminatory laws and supported educational initiatives for Black children.

One of the most defining moments in Loguen's life came in 1851, when the United States passed the Fugitive Slave Act. This law, which was designed to undermine the efforts of abolitionists, created a safety and legal dilemma for many who had been sheltering runaway slaves.

Loguen, who by this point had become a prominent figure in Syracuse, New York, made an audacious decision: he would defy the law. In 1851, a group of slave-catchers arrived in Syracuse with the intention of capturing two enslaved individuals who had escaped from their owners. Loguen, knowing they were under his protection, took a stand. When the slave-catchers demanded the return of the fugitives, Loguen stood firm. In a dramatic act of defiance, he led a crowd of his supporters to the courthouse, where the fugitives were being held, and forcibly freed them.

This act of rebellion against the Fugitive Slave Act was a momentous event in both Loguen's life and in the broader abolitionist movement. It became a symbol of resistance, showing that the laws of the United States would not be upheld if they contradicted basic human rights. Loguen's bold actions ignited a wave of similar acts of defiance in the North and further cemented his legacy as one of the great abolitionists of his time.

After the Civil War and the abolition of slavery in 1865, Loguen continued his work as a minister and community leader. He remained active in advocating for the rights of African Americans during the Reconstruction era, particularly in relation to issues such as land ownership, voting rights, and education. However, as a result of his deep involvement in the anti-slavery movement, he had to constantly contend with racism and prejudice, even in the supposedly free states.

In his later years, Loguen moved to Canada, where he lived for the remainder of his life. He continued to be involved in the fight for freedom and equality until his death in 1872. Today, Loguen's name lives on in the annals of American history as a hero of the abolitionist movement. His contributions to the Underground Railroad and his fearless resistance to slavery have made him a symbol of the unyielding struggle for liberty.

Jermain Wesley Loguen's life was a testament to the power of one individual's actions to change the course of history. Born into slavery, he rose to become a leading figure in the fight for liberation, both as a conductor of the Underground Railroad and as an outspoken advocate for the rights of African Americans. His

293

commitment to justice, his courage in the face of danger, and his unwavering belief in the equality of all people make him one of the most remarkable figures of the abolitionist era. Today, Loguen's legacy endures, reminding us that the fight for freedom and justice is never truly over, and that individuals, even in the face of insurmountable odds, can change the world.

Our Nig; Sketches from the Life of a Free Black: Harriet E. Wilson 1859

Harriet E. Wilson (1825–1900) occupies a unique and often overlooked place in American literary history. She was the first African American woman to publish a novel in the United States, a remarkable achievement considering the oppressive social and racial barriers that African Americans—particularly women—faced in the 19th century. Wilson's novel, *Our Nig: or, Sketches from the Life of a Free Black*, published in 1859, stands as one of the earliest works of African American literature and a poignant depiction of race, class, and gender in antebellum America.

Though her work was largely forgotten for many decades, recent scholarship has resurrected Wilson's legacy and recognized her contribution to the literary canon. This chapter seeks to explore the life and impact of Harriet E. Wilson, a woman whose story was nearly lost to history but who, through her writing, gave voice to the struggles of Black women in a deeply divided and unjust society.

Harriet E. Wilson was born in New Hampshire in 1825 to an enslaved mother, Rachel, and a white father. Her birth is often noted as one of the few known instances of a child born to a Black woman and a white man in New England during the period, where racial hierarchies were rigidly enforced. As an infant, Wilson was separated from her mother and

295

placed in the care of her father's relatives. This separation marked the beginning of a challenging and tumultuous childhood, one that would later inform the themes of abandonment, identity, and survival that would run through her novel.

At the age of 8, Wilson was orphaned after her mother died, and she was placed in an abusive household. She was sent to live with a white family in New Hampshire, who treated her harshly. This experience of neglect, emotional cruelty, and racial prejudice shaped her views on the realities of life as a Black person in the North—a region that prided itself on being free, but still harbored deep racial prejudice. Wilson's experience was not uncommon for Black children in the North during the era, where free Blacks often lived in poverty and faced systemic racism despite their freedom from enslavement.

By her teenage years, Wilson had witnessed and experienced firsthand the brutalities and limitations of being both Black and female. She struggled to find stability, ultimately working as a servant and experiencing poverty and neglect throughout her early adulthood. She married a man named James Wilson, though their union was strained, and her struggles continued.

In the mid-1850s, Harriet E. Wilson found herself living in Boston and experiencing the challenges that came with being an African American woman in a society that marginalized her on multiple fronts. Drawing on her own experiences of abuse, separation, and racial injustice, she wrote *Our Nig: or, Sketches from the Life of a Free Black*, which was published in 1859

296

under the pseudonym "H.E. Wilson." The novel was marketed as a work of fiction, though many scholars believe it was based on Wilson's own life experiences.

Our Nig is considered one of the first novels by an African American woman, and it is a groundbreaking work in the genre of African American literature. The novel tells the story of Frado, a young Black girl who is abandoned by her mother and sent to live with a white family in the North. Frado experiences mistreatment and exploitation at the hands of her "mistress," much like Wilson had experienced herself as a child. The novel deals with themes of racial identity, class, and gender, offering a sharp critique of the social structures that allowed such abuses to take place.

One of the novel's most remarkable features is its portrayal of the complexity of race relations in the North. Unlike the South, where slavery was overt and institutionalized, the North's treatment of African Americans was often more insidious—exclusion, discrimination, and a rigid class system that relegated free Black people to a status of second-class citizenship. Wilson's novel serves as a critique of the supposedly "free" North, where even free African Americans were often subjected to prejudice and exploitation.

The book also delves into the struggles of Black women, who faced the intersection of racial and gendered oppression. Frado's experiences of mistreatment at the hands of both white people and Black men highlight how Black women were doubly marginalized, existing at the intersection of racial and gender inequality. Wilson's portrayal of Frado's emotional and physical suffering offers a voice to Black women who were too often rendered invisible in the literary and social landscapes of the time.

Upon its publication, *Our Nig* did not receive widespread attention, and Wilson's authorship of the book was largely ignored by mainstream literary circles. It was marketed primarily to a white audience and didn't receive the recognition it deserved during Wilson's lifetime. In fact, after its initial publication, the novel went out of print, and Wilson's name was largely forgotten by the time of her death in 1900.

However, in the mid-20th century, scholars began to rediscover Wilson's work. *Our Nig* was reprinted in 1983 by Beacon Press, bringing attention to Wilson's story and positioning her as an important precursor to the Harlem Renaissance and the broader African American literary tradition. It became clear that Wilson's novel was not just a personal memoir but an important contribution to the canon of American literature, offering a sharp critique of racial and gendered oppression.

Wilson's work was a precursor to later African American authors who would explore themes of racial identity, gender, and social injustice, including Zora Neale Hurston, Toni Morrison, and Maya Angelou. The novel's ability to address the nuances of Black life in the 19th century—especially the experience of Black women—was a profound contribution that added depth to the understanding of American slavery, freedom, and racial identity.

Though Harriet E. Wilson did not achieve recognition in her own time, her contribution to African American literature is now widely acknowledged. She was an early voice in a growing tradition of Black writers.

Nicholas "Nick" Biddle: A soldier's soldier 1861

Nicholas "Nick" Biddle stands as a quiet testament to the resilience and spirit of a man who carved a path for himself in a nation on the brink of collapse. Born in 1796, Biddle was not merely a victim of circumstance but an individual who rose above the brutal realities of slavery, fought for the Union, and became the first person to be wounded by hostile action in the American Civil War. His story is one of struggle, survival, and an unyielding dedication to the ideals of freedom and patriotism that would eventually define the nation.

Nick Biddle's early life began in the heart of the South, amidst the oppression and violence of slavery. Born in Delaware, an enslaved man in a state where the institution of slavery still clung to its roots even as it became one of the border states during the Civil War, Biddle's early years were marked by toil, subjugation, and the constant yearning for freedom.

By his early twenties, Biddle had managed to escape the shackles of slavery, a feat that required cunning, bravery, and a deep belief in the possibility of a life beyond the chains that had held him captive. The details of his escape remain largely unknown, but like so many other men and women of his time, Biddle sought to make a life for himself in free territory, settling in Schuylkill County, Pennsylvania, where he would become an integral part of his new community.

Biddle's new life was not one of isolation; he built relationships and established a reputation in the community. He became well-known, and his hard work and determination earned him respect. His path would eventually intersect with the growing conflict in America— the Civil War—and he would find himself part of a larger struggle that would transform the nation.

In 1861, as the nation teetered on the brink of war, Biddle, now a free man, felt the pull to serve the Union cause. At the outbreak of the Civil War, Pennsylvania, with its strong abolitionist sentiment, became a hotbed for volunteer regiments. Many African Americans, particularly those like Biddle, eager to protect their hard-won freedom and prevent the spread of slavery, enlisted in both official military units and local militia companies.

Biddle joined the Washington Artillery, a militia company under the command of Captain James Wren. While not yet fully recognized as an official unit within the U.S. Army, these volunteers were crucial in the early stages of the war. Biddle, now an orderly, was tasked with logistical duties, supporting the regiment and aiding in any way he could. Though unarmed and not fully part of the military structure, he remained steadfast in his commitment, driven by the same sense of duty that fueled many young men eager to defend the Union.

On April 18, 1861, just days after the first shots were fired at Fort Sumter, Biddle's life would take a fateful turn. He and other unarmed volunteers were part of a group traveling to

301

Washington, D.C., to join the federal forces in their preparation for war. As they made their way through Baltimore, a city known for its divided loyalties, a pro-Confederate mob ambushed the group.

The mob, furious at the sight of Union soldiers marching through what they saw as Confederate territory, attacked the volunteers with ferocity. Biddle was struck in the head by a brick, the blow so severe that it exposed the bone in his skull. It was a brutal and unprovoked act of violence, and Biddle's injury marked him as the first Union soldier to be wounded in the conflict.

The pain from the injury was excruciating, but Biddle, even in his suffering, remained focused on the mission at hand. He was carried along with the other wounded soldiers to a nearby train, which transported them to Washington, D.C., where the gravity of the nation's war would soon be felt by all.

Biddle's injury, though grave, did not end his service. His recovery was slow and painful, but he remained committed to the cause. The scar left on his head became a permanent reminder of his sacrifice and a symbol of his patriotism. Biddle, in many ways, wore this injury with pride, describing it as a "military badge and brand of patriotism." To him, it was not merely a wound but a testament to the cause he had joined—the fight for freedom and the abolition of slavery.

Throughout the course of his recovery, Biddle remained with the Washington Artillery, continuing to serve the full three-month term of his enlistment. His determination to stay with the regiment despite his injury was a reflection of his deep belief in the Union cause. The men of the regiment, recognizing Biddle's bravery and sacrifice, took up a collection to ensure that his grave would be properly marked after his death— a fitting tribute to a man who had given so much.

By 1864, Biddle had returned to civilian life in Schuylkill County, where his reputation as a war hero had only grown. He was no longer just a man of the community; he was now a symbol of the Union's struggle and a living testament to the price of freedom. In that same year, Biddle participated in the Great Central Fair in Philadelphia, an event designed to raise funds for wounded Union soldiers. He sold his photograph at the fair, with the proceeds going directly to the care of the men who, like him, had suffered on the battlefield.

This act of charity spoke to Biddle's ongoing commitment to the cause. Though the war was far from over, he recognized that even after the battlefield was silent, there would still be work to do—helping those who had been wounded, both physically and psychologically, by the conflict. His efforts to raise money for the wounded soldiers reflected the deep sense of solidarity that united those who had fought for the Union, a brotherhood that transcended race and background.

As the war came to a close, Biddle's life continued quietly in Pennsylvania. He was regarded with deep respect by those who knew him, and his name became synonymous with bravery and sacrifice. In recognition of his service, the men of the Washington Artillery and the National Light Infantry raised money to provide a proper headstone for Biddle's grave at Bethel AME Church in Pottsville, Pennsylvania. This final gesture ensured that his legacy would not be forgotten.

When Nick Biddle passed away in 1876, the nation was forever changed. The war he had participated in had abolished slavery, and his participation in that cause was an integral part of the larger story of America's evolution. Though Biddle may not have been a famous general or politician, his role in the Civil War, and particularly his status as the first person wounded by hostile action, cemented his place in history. The scar on his forehead remained a symbol of his devotion to the Union and his deep belief in the cause of freedom.

Nick Biddle's story is a reminder that the struggle for justice and freedom is often fought by unsung heroes, men and women who, like him, fought not for recognition, but for the simple belief that all people deserved liberty. His life, scarred by war but filled with unshakeable conviction, remains a testament to the resilience of the human spirit and the power of self-determination.

A Freedman's Request for Thirty-Two Years of Back Wages: Jordan Anderson 1865

The Civil War had ended in 1865, and with it came the promise of freedom for four million enslaved African Americans who had been liberated from bondage. However, freedom for former slaves was often a complex and precarious reality. Many former slaves, having lived for generations in a system that dehumanized them, found that the fight for freedom did not end with the abolition of slavery. For some, the lingering ties of dependence, fear, and survival made the transition to liberty difficult and fraught with tension.

One of the most poignant and powerful expressions of this complex relationship between former slaves and their former masters is a letter written by Jordan Anderson, a former enslaved man, to his former owner, Colonel P.H. Anderson, in 1865. The letter is a remarkable document, as it not only expresses the dignity and determination of a newly freed man, but also encapsulates the tensions of Reconstruction, the aftermath of the Civil War, and the ongoing struggle for racial equality.

In this chapter, we will examine the background, context, and content of Jordan Anderson's letter, exploring its historical significance and its lasting impact as a testament to the strength and courage of those who sought to redefine their lives after emancipation.

Jordan Anderson was born into slavery in the early 1800s in Tennessee, a slaveholding state in the South. He worked on the plantation of Colonel P.H. Anderson, a wealthy landowner, where he labored as a field hand, along with his wife, Amanda, and children. Anderson, like many enslaved people, was subjected to the brutal conditions of slavery, which deprived him of his freedom and basic human rights.

In 1864, as the Civil War raged, Jordan Anderson, like many other enslaved people, seized the opportunity presented by the Union army's advances into Southern territory. He and his family escaped from the Anderson plantation, seeking refuge with the Union forces in Nashville, Tennessee. They joined the large numbers of enslaved people who fled their masters, hoping to secure their freedom with the advancing Northern armies.

While Jordan Anderson's journey to freedom was part of the larger mass exodus of enslaved people during the Civil War, his story would not end with mere escape. In 1865, following the Union's victory and the passage of the Thirteenth Amendment, which abolished slavery in the United States, the newly freed African Americans faced a new and uncertain world. For Jordan, the end of the war brought not only a sense of relief, but also the opportunity to settle down, reunite with his family, and start a new life.

However, in the same year, Jordan received an unexpected and remarkable letter from his former owner, Colonel P.H. Anderson. The letter, which was written by the Colonel, requested that Jordan return to the plantation to resume his work. The former master, it seemed, had fallen on hard times after the war and hoped to rehire Jordan, who was still considered an "employee" in the eyes of his old master. It was an offer made in the context of the profound social, economic, and political upheaval of the post-war South.

The request, however, was not a simple plea for labor; it was laden with the complex and painful realities of post-slavery relationships. It was a letter that presumed a certain level of obligation, one that disregarded the fact that Jordan Anderson had, for the first time in his life, experienced freedom. Jordan's response would not only reveal his personal determination and dignity but also serve as a public statement about the very nature of freedom and the ongoing struggle for Black equality in America.

On August 7, 1865, Jordan Anderson, now a free man, wrote a letter in reply to his former master's request. The letter was addressed directly to Colonel Anderson, and it is considered one of the most powerful documents of the Reconstruction era.

The letter was written with a calm and measured tone, but underneath the polite phrasing lay a powerful message of autonomy, self-respect, and dignity. Jordan's reply began with an acknowledgment of Colonel Anderson's request, but he immediately made clear his position on the matter of returning to the plantation.

"I take the opportunity of answering your letter, which I suppose is to be a good one, and I do not doubt that you would have been glad to have me back," Jordan began, acknowledging the letter but with a careful distance. However, the heart of his response lay in his candid enumeration of his reasons for not returning to the plantation.

Jordan continued, "I am at present living in freedom and have been living in it for a number of years now. I wish to continue to live in that freedom, and I do not wish to return to the chains that you once bound me with. The best way to preserve my freedom is to stay here, in the land of liberty."

This was not just a personal declaration; it was a statement about the nature of the new reality for former slaves. No longer were they bound by the chains of slavery, nor were they beholden to the whims of a former master. Jordan was asserting his right to live freely, as a man, and to choose his own future.

But perhaps the most striking part of the letter was Jordan's candid assessment of Colonel Anderson's request. Jordan acknowledged that his former master had been kind to him in some ways, but he was unequivocal in his insistence that his freedom was non-negotiable.

"I do not owe you anything, nor do I owe any part of my life to you. I do not wish to return to a life of servitude, and I do not need to ask for your permission to live free," he wrote.

308

Jordan's letter was deeply personal, yet it resonated with broader themes of freedom, equality, and dignity. In many ways, it echoed the sentiments of the larger abolitionist movement, which had long championed the cause of emancipation and civil rights for African Americans. Jordan's refusal to return to the plantation was not just an individual decision; it was an assertion of his newfound humanity and a rejection of the system of slavery that had defined his life for so long.

Jordan Anderson's letter to Colonel P.H. Anderson is often regarded as one of the most eloquent expressions of the challenges and complexities of freedom in the post-Civil War South. His decision to write the letter, and the content of his response, captures the transformation that African Americans experienced in the aftermath of emancipation.

For Jordan, freedom was not just a legal status—it was a moral and psychological assertion of his humanity. The very fact that he could write a letter, speak his mind, and refuse to return to the place where he had been held in bondage was a revolutionary act. His response was a rejection of the paternalism that many Southern whites continued to try to impose on Black people in the Reconstruction era. It was also a clear message that the promises of freedom and equality, while still unrealized in many ways, were now something that African Americans would defend with determination.

The letter is also significant because it was not just an expression of personal sentiment—it was a public one. Jordan's reply was not only addressed to Colonel Anderson but to the broader world that was still grappling with the question of how to treat freed people. It underscored the fact that emancipation did not mean the end of racial inequality or discrimination, but rather the beginning of a new and difficult struggle for African Americans to claim their rightful place as equals in American society.

Jordan Anderson's letter is a reminder of the resilience and courage of Black Americans in the face of adversity. It stands as a testament to the determination of freed people to assert their rights and dignity in a country that had long denied them both. Though the letter itself may not have been widely circulated in its time, its significance has grown over the years as historians, educators, and activists have come to recognize its powerful message about the true meaning of freedom.

For Jordan Anderson, the letter marked the beginning of a new life, one in which he could live as a free man, with his family, his dignity, and his rights intact. His words are a lasting testament to the struggles and victories of the African American experience during the Reconstruction era—a period that, though often fraught with challenges, laid the foundation for future generations to continue the fight for equality and justice.

Jordan Anderson's letter to his former master is a document that encapsulates the complexities of freedom in the wake of the Civil War. In it, we see not only the voice of a man asserting his autonomy and rejecting the remnants of his past life in bondage, but also the echoes of a larger struggle for racial equality and human dignity. The letter reminds us that freedom is not just a legal status but a profound, personal assertion of one's humanity—a sentiment that Jordan Anderson expressed with unparalleled clarity and strength. His letter remains one of the most compelling expressions of emancipation and should continue to inspire all who seek equitable justice.

Bibliography

"Slave Codes – Ulster County Truth and Reconciliation Commission." https://uctruthandrec.ulstercountyny.gov/slavecodes/.

"Uprisings and Rebellions: Armed Struggles against the Oppressive Institutions of Slavery, Colonialism, and Apartheid." *Oxford African American Studies Center*, December 1, 2006. https://doi.org/10.1093/acref/9780195301731.013.43737.

Banks, William M. *Black Intellectuals: Race and Responsibility in American Life*. 1st ed. W.W. Norton, 1996. https://catalog.libraries.psu.edu/catalog/1733966.

Bay, Mia, Farah Jasmine Griffin, Martha S. Jones, and Barbara Dianne Savage, eds. *Toward an Intellectual History of Black Women*. Chapel Hill: University of North Carolina Press, 2015.

Berlin, Ira. *Generations of Captivity: A History of African American Slaves*. Cambridge: Belknap Press of Harvard University Press, 2003.

Berlin, Ira. *Many Thousands Gone: The First Two Centuries of Slavery in North America*. Cambridge: Belknap Press of Harvard University Press, 1998.

Blackett, R. J. M. *Making Freedom: The Underground Railroad and the Politics of Slavery.* The University of North Carolina Press, 2013.

Blassingame, John W. *The Slave Community: Plantation Life in the Antebellum South.* New York: Oxford University Press, 1979.

Blight, David W., and Jim Downs, eds. *Beyond Freedom: Disrupting the History of Emancipation.* Athens: The University of Georgia Press, 2017.

Bogues, Anthony. *Black Heretics, Black Prophets: Radical Political Intellectuals.* Routledge, 2003. https://catalog.libraries.psu.edu/catalog/263 0591.

Cameron, Guy, and Stephen Vermette. "The Role of Extreme Cold in the Failure of the San Miguel de Gualdape Colony." *The Georgia Historical Quarterly* 96, no. 3 (Fall 2012): 291–307. http://www.jstor.org/stable/23622193.

Curto, José C., and Renée Soulodre-LaFrance, eds. *Africa and the Americas: Interconnections During the Slave Trade.* Trenton, NJ: Africa World Press, 2005.

Davidson, David M. "Negro Slave Control and Resistance in Colonial Mexico, 1519-1650." *The Hispanic American Historical Review* 46, no. 3 (August 1966): 235–53. https://doi.org/10.2307/2510626.

Du Bois, W. E. B. *Black Reconstruction in America*. New York: The Free Press, 1998.

Dunbar, Erica Armstrong. *Never Caught: The Washingtons' Relentless Pursuit of Their Runaway Slave, Ona Judge*. New York: 37 Ink, 2018.

Foner, Eric. *Reconstruction: America's Unfinished Revolution, 1863-1877*. New York: HarperPerennial, 2014.

Foreman, P. Gabrielle, Jim Casey, and Sarah Lynn Patterson, eds. *The Colored Conventions Movement: Black Organizing in the Nineteenth Century*. Chapel Hill: The University of North Carolina Press, 2021.

Genovese, Eugene D. *Roll, Jordan, Roll: The World the Slaves Made*. New York: Vintage Books, 1976.

Hahn, Steven. *A Nation Under Our Feet: Black Political Struggles in the Rural South from Slavery to the Great Migration*. Cambridge: Belknap, 2005.

Hoey, Edwin. "Terror in New York - 1741." *American Heritage* 25, no. 4 (June 1974).

Hoffman, Paul E. *A New Andalucia and a Way to the Orient: The American Southeast during the Sixteenth Century*. Baton Rouge: Louisiana State University Press, 2015.

Holden, Vanessa M. *Surviving Southampton: African American Women and*

Resistance in Nat Turner's Community. Urbana: University of Illinois Press, 2021.

Horne, Gerald. *The Counter-Revolution of 1776: Slave Resistance and the Origins of the United States of America.* New York: New York University Press, 2014.

Johnson, J.G. "A SPANISH SETTLEMENT IN CAROLINA, 1526." *The Georgia Historical Quarterly* 7, no. 4 (December 1923): 339–45. http://www.jstor.org/stable/40575769.

Johnson, Walter. *River of Dark Dreams: Slavery and Empire in the Cotton Kingdom.* Belknap Press of Harvard University Press, 2013. https://catalog.libraries.psu.edu/catalog/9486948.

Johnson, Walter. *Soul by Soul: Life Inside the Antebellum Slave Market.* Cambridge: Harvard University Press, 1999.

Landers, Jane. "Africans in the Spanish Colonies." *Historical Archaeology*, Diversity and Social Identity in Colonial Spanish America: Native American, African, and Hispanic Communities during the Middle Period, 31, no. 1 (1997): 84–103. https://www.jstor.org/stable/25616520.

Love, Edgar F. "Negro Resistance to Spanish Rule in Colonial Mexico." *The Journal of Negro History* 52, no. 2 (April 1967): 89–103. https://doi.org/10.2307/2716127.

Makalani, Minkah. *In the Cause of Freedom: Radical Black Internationalism from Harlem to London, 1917-1939.* University of North Carolina Press, 2011. https://catalog.libraries.psu.edu/catalog/194 83581.

Manning, Chandra. *Troubled Refuge: Struggling for Freedom in the Civil War.* New York: Vintage Books, 2017.

Miller, Floyd J. *The Search for a Black Nationality: Black Emigration and Colonization, 1787-1863.* University of Illinois Press, 1975. https://catalog.libraries.psu.edu/catalog/120 9614.

Morgan, Edmund S. *American Slavery, American Freedom: The Ordeal of Colonial Virginia.* New York: W.W. Norton & Co., 2003.

Oakes, James. *Freedom National: The Destruction of Slavery in the United States, 1861-1865.* New York: W.W. Norton & Co., 2013.

Peck, Douglas T. "Lucas Vásquez de Ayllón's Doomed Colony of San Miguel de Gualdape." *The Georgia Historical Quarterly* 85, no. 2 (Summer 2001): 183–98. https://www.jstor.org/stable/40584407.

Quigley, Paul, ed. *The Civil War and the Transformation of American Citizenship.* Baton Rouge: Louisiana State University Press, 2018.

Redkey, Edwin S. *Black Exodus: Black Nationalist and Back-to-Africa Movements,*

1890-1910. New Haven: Yale University Press, 1969.

Robinson, Cedric J. *Black Movements in America*. New York: Routledge, 1997.

Rockman, Seth. *Scraping By: Wage Labor, Slavery, and Survival in Early Baltimore*. Baltimore: Johns Hopkins University Press, 2009.

Rucker, Walter C. *The River Flows On: Black Resistance, Culture, and Identity Formation in Early America*. Louisiana paperback ed. Antislavery, Abolition, and the Atlantic World. Baton Rouge: Louisiana State University Press, 2007.

Rucker, Walter. "Westmoreland Slave Plot (1687)." In *Encyclopedia Virginia*. Virginia Foundation for the Humanities, 2011. https://encyclopediavirginia.org/entries/westmoreland-slave-plot-1687/.

Schneider, Dorothy, and Carl J. Schneider. *Slavery in America*. Rev. ed. New York: Facts on File, 2008.

Sinha, Manisha. *The Slave's Cause: A History of Abolition*. New Haven: Yale University Press, 2016.

Smallwood, Stephanie E. *Saltwater Slavery: A Middle Passage from Africa to American Diaspora*. Cambridge: Harvard University Press, 2008.

Spires, Derrick Ramon. *The Practice of Citizenship: Black Politics and Print Culture in*

317

the Early United States. Philadelphia: University of Pennsylvania Press, 2019.

Torres-Spelliscy, Ciara. "Everyone Is Talking about 1619. But That's Not Actually When Slavery in America Started." *The Washington Post*, August 23, 2019. https://www.washingtonpost.com/outlook/2019/08/23/everyone-is-talking-about-thats-not-actually-when-slavery-america-started/.

Waters, Kristin, and Carol B. Conaway, eds. *Black Women's Intellectual Traditions: Speaking Their Minds*. Waltham: Brandeis University Press, 2022.

Whites, LeeAnn. *Gender Matters: Civil War, Reconstruction, and the Making of the New South*. New York: Palgrave Macmillan, 2005.

Wood, Peter H. *Black Majority: Negroes in Colonial South Carolina from 1670 through the Stono Rebellion*. New York: Norton, 1996.

Wood, Peter H. *Strange New Land: Africans in Colonial America*. Oxford: Oxford University Press, 2003.